Barefoot on Barbed Wire

CINDY MORGAN

HARVEST HOUSE PUBLISHERS
Eugene, Oregon 97402

BAREFOOT ON BARBED WIRE
Copyright © 2001 by Cindy Morgan
Published by Harvest House Publishers
Eugene, Oregon 97402

Library of Congress Cataloging-in-Publication Data
Morgan, Cindy, 1968–
    Barefoot on barbed wire / Cindy Morgan.
        p. cm.
    ISBN 0-7369-0095-0
        1. Morgan, Cindy, 1968–   . 2. Fear—Religious aspects—Christianity. I. Title.
BV4908.5.M66 2001
277.3'0825'092—dc21
[B]   00-063473

Printed in the United States of America

01 02 03 04 05 06 07 / BP-CF / 10 9 8 7 6 5 4 3 2

To Mama:
Welcome to the new world.
I love you.

Acknowledgments

All my heartfelt thanks to:
—Carolyn McCready for being so patient, full of inspiration, and unbelievably kind.

—Terry Glaspey for your invaluable touch as an editor; you have a wonderful gift.

—Bob Hawkins Jr., Betty Fletcher, Barb Sherrill, Stacey Hausler, Kim Moore, and all the amazing people at Harvest House. I am so proud to be associated with you.

—My sister Sam for walking through these pages with me—you are an amazing person.

—Sigmund, for being the kind of husband who does the dishes when I'm too tired, who feeds our baby and lets me sleep, and for being the best friend and the deepest love of my life.

Contents

Barefoot on Barbed Wire

When I was still a little girl, every summer my mom would make my sisters and me climb to the top of my grandpa's mountain, where he had a small two-room cabin. Just beyond his cabin was a field wild with blackberries ripe for the picking.

I always dreaded this yearly trek. We would be surrounded by the hum of a thousand jar flies, the bees buzzing about from one bush to another, and the humidity of a southern summer, hanging in the air as thick as honey.

Though I loved the taste of fresh butter and wild blackberry jam spread over my mom's cathead biscuits, it still just didn't seem worth it.

Truth is, I was afraid.

Several fears confronted me every time we made the trip up to the blackberry fields.

First, I was allergic to bee stings. Not enough to endanger my life, but enough to make me swell up in misery.

Second, blackberry bushes are a favorite hiding place for all kinds of snakes. My mother had no fear of snakes of any kind, but this fearlessness was not something that was passed down to me.

But most of all, I was afraid of what separated my grandfather's acreage from the blackberry field: a tall barbed wire fence.

Being a chubby and not particularly agile young girl, the prospect of squeezing myself between the rows of that razor-sharp barbed wire terrified me, causing me to break out in a cold sweat. My mouth went dry even thinking about it.

FEAR IS A STRANGE THING. It's hard to figure out where our fears come from and why each of us struggles with different fears. Why is it, for example, that my brother Mike can revel in skydiving and hang gliding while others are so frightened by even modest heights?

It's not simply a matter of heritage and example.

My mother is one of the most fearless people I know. She once refused to let my dad shoot a big black snake that had somehow made its way into the living room of our small log cabin. My sisters and I had climbed up on the kitchen table, out of harm's way, and were yelling for my father to "Shoot it! Shoot it!" My mother wouldn't hear of it, saying that it was just a black snake and that it would "only make you a little sick if it bit you."

I HAVE BEEN AFRAID OF MANY THINGS in my life and have struggled with all kinds of fear. I have found it hard to trust and to take risks, always afraid of what lay curled up around the next corner like that big black snake. My imagination can usually be counted on to dream up the worst possible scenario to any situation in my life.

I want to take risks, but sometimes my fear seems to conquer me. I just want to lie on the floor and close my eyes until the battle is over, until it all goes away.

Looking back on the years I spent in such bondage to fear makes me grateful to realize that I have come a long way in my journey to overcome it. I've learned that fear, in itself, is not always a bad thing. In the right proportion it guards and protects us from harm. But it can also bear bitter fruit in our lives, taking root in our hearts, growing into something that overwhelms and paralyzes us.

There are two kinds of stories I have to tell: First, I want to share some moments from my own journey toward overcoming fear. It is my hope and prayer that by understanding a little of my journey toward overcoming fear that some light will be cast upon another's path. Second, I'd like to share some moments from my life that are full of longing and wonder, the kind of moments that make me grateful to be alive. These moments remind me not to take for granted the most wonderful gift God has given me: my own life.

They remind me of what life looks like when I am not afraid.

Instead of focusing on my fears, I am learning to focus on the wonder, the longing, and the beauty of life. They remind me of what life looks like when I'm not afraid.

FOR ME, THE BARBED WIRE IS A SYMBOL of my risk and my fear.

I imagine kicking my shoes off on a hot summer day and roaming through the woods, splashing through a mountain stream, and coming upon a fence that I must cross to get to the other side, where a field of wildflowers wait.

The aroma draws me, so I bend the wire and I bow my back, risking that the sharp barbs might cut me. I know that I might be pricked and that I might bleed. But I will not be afraid.

Every scar that was once a wound is now a symbol of victory.

I raise my eyes to the sky and feel the warm sun breaking through the dark clouds—I taste the scent of freedom in the air. It gives me courage to trust—and to go barefoot on barbed wire.

Awakening

You are so negative."

It was a Sunday afternoon and we were newly married, living in a small duplex in Nashville, Tennessee. I had been complaining about something. I can't even remember what it was, but I was totally stressing out, sure that the world was going to come to an end over whatever dilemma I was facing that day.

Something I said pushed Sigmund over the edge. He stopped what he was doing and sat down next to me on the couch, taking my face between his hands and looking me straight in the eye. Gently, but firmly he spoke these words: "You are so negative."

I couldn't deny it. I knew he was right.

I MARRIED AN OPTIMIST.

Sigmund always sees the positive side to every situation, always looks for the good in people. From his view the glass is always half full.

But I knew it was not an empty optimism that caused him to speak the words that cut me to the quick. But I started to defend myself anyway, "What? I'm not..."

"You always react to a difficult situation by assuming the worst," he answered.

"But I..."

A concerned look came over his face. "What can we do to help you see the positive instead of the negative?"

I didn't know what to say. I just sat there in stunned silence because his words had finally penetrated into this thick skull of mine.

"You're right," I finally choked out, "I *am* negative."

That moment was a breakthrough.

THIS EXPERIENCE LED ME TO BEGIN to examine my life. What I realized about myself is that my whole life had been one long battle with fear.

Fear of failure.

Fear of rejection.

Fear that I would never measure up.

Fear that others would let me down.

Fear of death.

The enemy of my soul had trapped me in a desperate cycle of fear, made me feel defeated in every situation before I'd even had a chance to begin. My negativity came from the fear that I would be defeated by every obstacle that stood in my way.

One of the things that has helped me to break free from fear is a book I discovered the same afternoon that Sigmund lovingly helped me realize the extent of my problem. M. Blaine Smith's *The Optimism Factor* helped me understand that optimism is not just some sort of cheery wishful thinking, but that it is really just another word for faith.

God wants us to see beyond the struggle we are in, to not be afraid of the obstacles that present themselves to us. He wants us to understand that He will be with us, if only we'll let Him. It is possible for us to conquer our fears through our trust in God's power and love. The apostle Paul, imprisoned and facing death, was able, even in those circumstances, to feel the joy of the Lord (2 Timothy 4:18).

I AM BEGINNING TO CONQUER some of the fears that have haunted my life, to trust God and find His joy in every moment of my days.

Not long ago, if I was facing a forty-city tour, I would immediately start imagining the worst scenarios. I would probably lose my voice or else I would get sick and have to cancel concerts. Something bad was certain to happen.

Now I am learning to take the days one at a time.

I realized that I did better when I didn't look at the calendar. If I did, I'd become overwhelmed. I'd start worrying and feeling afraid. Instead, I let things come one at a time and trust God to be with me—through good situations and bad.

FEAR IS A THIEF.

It robs you of a happy future. It also robs you of the moment that is before you.

I wasted too many years being anxious, panicked, and fearful and lost thousands of potentially wonderful moments along the way.

If you too are in a struggle with fear, I hope you can learn the lesson I am learning: God can accomplish great things when we live our lives with open hands and an open heart.

He will take care of you.

He will be with you.

Instead of a life full of half-empty glasses, He offers us a life filled with living water, water that will quench our thirsty souls.

A Genealogy of Fear

When did my own journey with fear begin?
As a teen?
A child?
In the womb?
Or did it begin even earlier?
Somewhere far back in my family tree...

WHEN I THINK ABOUT THE WOMEN in my family, I am
inclined to believe that my struggle with fear is part of my
family heritage.

I think of my great-grandmother. We called her "Granny
Alice." I can remember being afraid of her from a very early
age, even though we'd never met. There had been too
many crazy stories about her swapped around the dinner
table not to arouse curiosity and fear in my young heart at
the prospect of meeting her.

On a scorching summer day, my family journeyed to her small house that sat nestled in the woods of a Kentucky hillside. I was a shy and quiet little eight-year-old girl and today I would finally be introduced to my great-grandmother.

Her house was rather primitive, worn grey from many years of weather and a lack of paint. On the porch there sat a large, silver-colored aluminum bucket filled with cold spring water. In it was a metal dipper that could be used to dip water out. I was thirsty from the long trip, so I plunged the dipper into the bucket and drew out a mouthful of water. When I raised it to my lips, I found it to be sweet and cold and refreshing.

It would be the only pleasant memory from this trip.

I looked up from my drink to my first glance at Granny Alice. She looked stern and unfriendly. I was soon to learn that this first impression was pretty accurate. Her hair was twisted tightly into a bun on the top of her head. It had lost its color long ago and was now the same silvery color as the bucket on her porch.

Her house was small, modest in every way, but neat and clean. Colorful patchwork quilts decorated the chairs and beds.

But what the house lacked was warmth, even on a hot summer day.

THE ADULTS FELL TO TALKING and I fell quiet.

Then I decided I needed to use the bathroom, but Granny Alice didn't have one inside her house. In fact, she had no indoor plumbing whatsoever.

I stepped off the porch and followed the well-worn path to a small outhouse that seemed to be leaning a little to one side. Finishing my business there, I pushed open the creaking wooden door and found Granny Alice standing there, staring down at me. Her look was deeply disapproving, as though I was some sort of spawn of Satan.

"Did you go and use all my toilet paper?" she demanded.

"No...I..."

"I can't stand wastefulness. This stuff is expensive. Give it to me!"

I meekly attempted to hand her what remained of the roll of toilet paper, but she jerked it out of my hands and carried it away close to her bosom, as though it were a baby or a bar of gold.

Looking back now, I figure that she was probably just afraid of not having enough, having been raised in extreme poverty and never having had much money.

But the fear of poverty was not her only fear. In fact, she was fearful of almost everything: fearful of sinning, fearful for her health, fearful of starving.

And from that day, I was fearful of *her*.

GRANNY ALICE'S DAUGHTER—my grandmother—inherited many things from her mother, including a mania for cleanliness. I remember clearly that her house was always filled with the pungent odor of Clorox. There was a reason for that—she washed everything in Clorox: the floors, the bathroom, the clothes, the dishes, the cups and glasses.

My grandmother was determined that no germ would take up shelter under her roof.

But where she differed from her mother was in her gentleness and sweet demeanor. She was always kind to me and all my brothers and sisters; her voice sweet and warm, and her sentences peppered with phrases like "I love you" and "Bless your heart." I always looked forward to talking with her on the phone or in person.

Looking back, though, I realize something I missed as a child: Grandma was filled with fear.

Though she was a strong and healthy woman, she was afraid.

She was afraid of change.

She was afraid of encountering anything unusual or different or unexpected.

She was afraid that someone might rob her house.

She was afraid that if she left the safety of her little house, she might not make it back home.

Consequently, she never left the small community where she lived and, in fact, rarely left her house, except to attend church, shop for groceries, or pay a visit to the doctor.

Her fear made her a prisoner in her own home.

Therefore, she never attended the weddings of her grandchildren or showed up for graduations or any other special occasions.

She was absent at all the most important moments of my life.

In fact, she didn't even attend the funeral of her own son-in-law, my father.

That was the hardest pill for me to swallow.

Even now, I find in myself an anger and bitterness toward her for her failure to be more involved in my life. I must deal with feelings of resentment because my relationship with her could never blossom or grow due to the paralyzing effect of her fear.

I'll never know what it would have been like to grow up with a special close relationship with my grandmother.

Is it too late?

Maybe not, but the bridge is long and the water beneath is deep.

And because of her fear, she can't even meet me halfway.

I ONCE HEARD A STORY ABOUT A WOMAN who was so afraid of someone breaking into her house that she put bars on every door and window. One night, while she was sleeping, a fire started. But she'd been so efficient at making it impossible for anyone to get in that she was also unable to escape herself. She died in her self-made prison.

I FEEL THE JANGLE OF THE CHAINS of fear that have haunted these generations of women in my family.

I see the reflection of those fears in my own eyes.

But I know the chain can be broken.

I must search beneath the surface. I must not be afraid to ask the hard questions—those that the women before me in my family could not bring themselves to ask.

It will not be easy.

But God never promised it would be easy, but He did promise that He would be with me.

Granny Alice

Wide Awake

My mother always had difficulty in sleeping.

We'd all be snug in our beds, covered with a dozen blankets to ward off the chill from the cold outside. Then we would hear one of two sounds: the sound of my mother's voice reading aloud from the Bible or the sound of her playing the piano. It was often about 2 A.M. when these sounds would come floating down the hallway, marking another bout of insomnia.

Neither sound was a very welcome treat, but you got used to it.

Was her problem plain, old-fashioned insomnia—or was it something deeper?

It is odd how a condition like that can come upon you without any warning.

ONLY A FEW YEARS AGO, I was living in Nashville in a small duplex in Sylvan Park, a quiet and relatively safe neighborhood. I knew almost everyone who lived around me and many of them were close friends. On any given night I could draw comfort from the safety in numbers.

But night became a terrifying time for me. After the sun went down I would begin to worry and feel fearful.

I thought that every sound, every creak of the floor was the footstep of someone coming to harm me.

Most nights I would climb the stairs to my bedroom, get into bed with my Bible close to me, and wait for the sounds that would paralyze me with fear. Finally, I would carefully tiptoe downstairs and push my couch against the front door. I'd make my futon into a bed and lie right there.

And had you been there you might have heard a sound that echoed what I had heard as a child. I would read the Bible aloud, in a voice just over a whisper.

I KNOW THAT MANY PEOPLE ARE scared to be by themselves sometimes, but for me it was a battle I fought every night for at least four years. I was only able to sleep without fear when, for periods of time, I would share my house with a roommate.

This struggle left me exhausted and weak, both physically and emotional.

Too afraid to sleep.

Too tired to stay awake.

I STILL DO BATTLE WITH THESE FEARS. When my husband is out of town, I can sometimes be found sitting bolt upright in bed, the only sound in the house being the riffling pages of my Bible.

It is my best weapon against my fear and a solace for my soul.

BUT WHAT KEPT MY MOTHER awake?

In her waking hours, she did not seem to be afraid of anything—not snakes or wild animals, and certainly not any boogie man or imaginary intruder.

Instead, she was afraid of the world she found when she closed her eyes, the world of dreams. It was a world that was unpredictable and full of questions.

It was a world she could not control.

Perhaps that is what makes fear so potent—the feeling that life itself is beyond our control. We cannot manage it or make it fit with our desires.

Maybe that is when it all comes down to trusting God.

Passing the Test

I don't think Mrs. Romine liked me.

There was to be a test in my fourth-grade science class and, as usual, I felt unprepared and unsure of the answers. My solution was to casually place my study paper between my legs, where I could refer to it whenever I was in need of an answer.

I knew it would look suspicious if I got a perfect score, so I was smart enough to answer a couple questions wrong on purpose—just to make it look good.

When the test was over, the papers were collected by our teacher, Mrs. Romine, a prudish, pinch-faced woman whose disposition made you wonder if she started out the day by adding pickle juice to her Cheerios rather than milk.

Mrs. Romine never liked me.

I wasn't too fond of her, either.

But as I watched her grade the papers, I figured I was home free.

I would not fail this test.

Suddenly, Mrs. Romine raised her head from what was obviously my paper and gave me a look that should have burned a hole through my skull. She pushed back her chair with a grating, screeching sound and strode purposefully to my desk, her eyes on me the entire time.

She hovered for a moment and then stared down at me.

"You received a 98 on this test," she said. "I find that very interesting. Would you mind if I quizzed you on a few of these questions?"

Cold beads of sweat started to appear on my forehead.

She rattled off the first question.

I stammered out an answer that was, of course, wrong.

She asked another, with a similar result.

Then another.

Finally, she leaned down into my face. I could feel her hot breath on my sweaty brow. She smiled an unpleasant smile, something like a smirk, and said, "You cheated, didn't you?"

My face turned as red as a firecracker.

With every eye in the class on me, I dropped my head in shame and told the painful truth.

"Yes, I cheated."

WHAT WOULD MAKE A SHY and usually honest girl cheat on a test? A girl who could normally be depended upon to tell the truth? Why did I take the risk? After all, straight As were never a goal that meant much to my parents. I guess I was just afraid of failure, afraid of letting other people down.

This fear has dogged me throughout my life.

For instance, I've always avoided group sports because I didn't want others depending on me. I was afraid I'd miss a pass or drop the ball at the worst possible moment and lose the game for my teammates.

So I've tended to stick to things that I can do solo, so that if I fail I only hurt myself. I've played it safe, never taking the risk of causing others to be disappointed in me, consequently failing often to push myself to be the best I could be.

BUT THE QUEST FOR PERFECTION IS an impossible goal. And it will cripple you if you seek after it.

My years in music have taught me that perfection is not the main element in a good performance. Even the most gifted singers, with the ability to perform with pristine perfection, can be disappointing if they lack two key elements: vulnerability and heart. Without these, their performance is cold and fails to touch the audience.

Whenever we make ourselves vulnerable and expose our heart, we will almost always make a few mistakes. That just comes with the territory. It has been my experience that the overall performance will be more satisfying, more enjoyable, because it will be more passionate.

Life is much the same.

When I focus on trying to live perfectly, trying to make sure everyone is happy with me and that everyone thinks I'm wonderful and deeply spiritual and amazingly gifted, the results are usually not pretty. I end up strangled by my fears. I cannot live up to this self-imposed standard.

When I focus on living with passion, however, I find myself connected to a place deep inside. When I live with passion I can live courageously, setting fear aside. And since we are all much the same inside—filled with insecurity and self-doubt—I find that others are touched by my willingness to be vulnerable. They see themselves in the mirror of imperfection that I hold out.

I can only overcome my fear of failing in the eyes of others by living from my passions and by trusting in God's grace to overcome the effects of my inadequacy. He can make the most of my shortcomings.

And though I couldn't count on Mrs. Romine for understanding and grace, I know I can always count on God.

Eight years old

Cabin in the holler

In These Rooms

When I was ten years old, my family moved from our small white house in Harrogate to a new home in the "Holler" (near Speedwell, Tennessee). Our old home held many memories of friendly neighbors and scraped knees, but we were ready to venture into a new life in the hills of Tennessee.

Our lives would never be the same.

It was like a dream, really, as we drove deep into a wilderness of trees on the small, one-lane dirt road that wound and meandered through the forest. From time to time we would pass a mountain spring and look up to see a gentle fall of water that trickled down from somewhere in the cliffs on the mountaintops.

Finally, we came to a large rusted metal gate that swung over a cattle guard. Passing through, we drove a bit farther down the road. The trees were thick on both sides, and it was kind of dark among them, but you could still glimpse a stream winding alongside. White water splashed over the rocks in the stream with a sound like muffled laughter. It looked like something from a dream. At twenty feet across, it looked too small to be a river and too large to be a creek.

As we drove, the sides of the road were lined with color and with the smell of honeysuckle.

Just when you thought you might never see the sky again, the trees opened like a large doorway into the heavens and there was our valley.

Golden and green.

A small log cabin was nestled in the valley, as though it was the center of the world. And for us, it was.

It was a world of bumblebees, alive and buzzing.

Of fields of wildflowers.

Of running water and plentiful crawdads.

A place for bare feet and dancing in the sunshine.

Crossing into the valley, we had entered into a world that felt like a special place, as if we were the first to discover it. It seemed a secret that God had kept and saved especially for us.

Inside the cabin was a cozy living room, where a large wagon wheel hung from a beam in the ceiling. A fireplace as wide as the room itself was built of rocks handpicked from the creek nearby.

The kitchen had a wood-burning stove, a stove that would soon fill the house with the smell of fried potatoes and fresh-baked biscuits. Next to the stove there was a little round table with a checkered cloth, a table that would soon groan under the load of abundant homemade meals.

My parents' bedroom was pretty good sized, spacious enough to fit their king-size bed, their dresser, and my mother's extensive collection of wigs. Two of my sisters shared a room next to Mom and Dad's, a room that was rumored to be the place where a woman who lived there previously had practiced witchcraft. We all agreed that we dreamed strange dreams when we slept in that room.

My room doubled as the laundry room, my bed sharing space with the washing machine. Though very small, it had a window perfect for daydreaming and for wondering at the world outside.

To save room and money, we hung our clothes out in the sunshine and on cold days let them dry by hanging them near the crackling fire in the living room.

We all settled happily into this cozy little cabin: my mom and dad, my sisters (Sam, Sherry, and Tammy), and me. Visits were frequent from relatives, especially my older brothers, Mike and Haze. The cozy little house seemed always filled with people I loved.

IN THESE ROOMS WE LOVED and laughed, shouted and cried.

It was home.

All too soon we would one by one leave the house to go our own way, slowly losing this lifeline to childhood and innocence.

From the comforting arms of this cabin we were eventually passed into the arms of the outer world, a world filled with knowledge and experiences that would ensnare and abuse us, that would shape us into the people we would become.

It is a road we all must travel, from the womb to the grave.

But for a while our world seemed perfect, lovely, and at peace. There in our cabin in the valley, in the place we would always call home.

Grandpa Burney
with his favorite shot gun

Grandpa's Mountain

My grandfather was a mountain man.

He lived in a two-room cabin that he and my father built together. It sat on the slope of a mountain that they had cleared and planted with seemingly endless rows of corn, green beans, tomatoes, cucumbers, potatoes, and lettuce.

Grandpa liked things simple.

He had no running water or electricity. He bathed in a galvanized steel tub. He had a wood-burning stove and used oil lanterns for light.

When we visited him, my dad would lead me and my sisters up the trail through the woods, each of us carrying a gallon of sloshing spring water. The water came from a spring at the foot of the mountain that gushed cold, sweet water. I can remember always seeing a little sand at the bottom of each jug. But this never bothered Grandpa.

As a matter of fact, the only thing that bothered Grandpa was the stress of living in the modern world. I guess that's why he chose to live at the top of a mountain without any modern conveniences.

It was a choice he made.

As we drew close to the cabin, we'd always find him working outside.

There was plenty to be done.

He chopped wood, tended his garden, and carried on conversations with Smokey, his large black dog, who bore a strong resemblance to a bear.

He was always laughing and happy to see us. We'd find him dressed in his usual outfit, a flannel shirt and overalls, looking very thin, but in excellent health. Around his waist he wore a pistol, hanging comfortably in a holster near his hip. I don't ever remember seeing him without that gun.

Grandpa spoke quietly, in a sort of mumble, but he'd smile and invite us in for dinner. He'd peel potatoes (he called them "taters") and fry them on top of his stove. He'd serve them with fresh green beans from his garden and the best corn bread you've ever tasted. It smelled good and tasted even better.

Sometimes we'd ask Grandpa to tell us a story about growing up or about his days as a moonshiner. But our favorite stories were the wild tales about his daughter, Willa Mae who, at her own insistence, was best known as "Aunt Bill."

When he started in on one of these stories about "Wild Bill," it was as if the rest of the world fell away. We were so happy there in that little cabin, listening intently as he spun his tale and a steady stream of smoke rose from the chimney and from the unfiltered Pall Malls he smoked. Dad would find a small chair in the corner and sip black coffee, smiling and laughing at every story my grandfather told.

We all felt transported to a world of fewer complications, a life simple and good, a life free of so many of the unnecessary trappings that romance us with their allure.

AT THE END OF OUR AFTERNOONS with him, we would be reluctant to leave, all of us wanting to savor every moment of the world we'd temporarily escaped to—the world of Grandpa's mountain.

As we descended the mountain, a gentle smile would reside on our faces as we remembered the stories, the wonderful food, and his incredible warmth. It was as though we'd stepped through a portal into another time, a time when life was good and simple and people could be trusted.

GRANDPA BARNEY IS STILL ALIVE. But he can no longer live by himself on the mountain. Those times live only in our memories. Now Grandpa lives in Ohio with my aunt, Sue.

As I write this, I am expecting my first child. I can't wait to visit him with his new great-granddaughter. I hope she too can hear him tell some of the stories I've cherished all these years.

I want her to see the sparkle in his eye and hear that infectious laugh, the laugh that always reminds me of the good times we had on Grandpa's mountain.

The Snake Juggler

Perhaps I should tell you a little something about "Wild Bill."

There were three houses in the Hollow where we lived: our house, Grandpa's cabin, and the house where my dad's sister lived.

Her name was Willa Mae, but she, as I said earlier, preferred to simply be called Bill. To me, she was always "Aunt Bill."

Aunt Bill led a colorful life. As a young girl she ran away from home to join the circus. She quickly made a name for herself as "The Snake Juggler." She traveled from city to city with the circus, and when her time came to perform she would dazzle audiences by juggling six rattlesnakes at one time. Although none of us were ever really sure how a person could juggle one snake—much less six of them—it certainly painted an amazing and mystifying picture in our minds.

Aunt Bill was never shy about telling the stories of all her escapades.

In fact, she wasn't shy about much of anything. Including her faith.

AUNT BILL WAS A SELF-PROCLAIMED Pentecostal preacher. She didn't feel the need for any ordination papers; she felt that God had called her to the ministry. That was good enough for her.

She was a voluptuous woman, whose jet-black hair fell as far as her waist. Her intense eyes were framed with glasses in the shape of cat's eyes, usually outlined with rhinestone studs. She wore floor-length skirts to match her hair. And her crowning glory was a sparkling gold tooth in the very center of her smile.

We were all fascinated by her...and a little afraid of her.

I NEVER ACTUALLY HEARD HER PREACH in a church, but I often overheard conversations about God between Aunt Bill and Mom. Mom was pretty liberated for that time and place and wholeheartedly approved of women preachers. Not everyone was so open-minded. Sometimes it could be an uphill battle for acceptance, but Aunt Bill was never one to shy away from a conflict.

Over the years I heard some pretty interesting stories about the adventures she'd had while preaching in little backwoods churches nestled high in the mountains of Tennessee, Virginia, and Kentucky.

These were churches where folklore and superstition were combined with a distorted version of Christianity.

There would often be a wooden box with a lid on it sitting at the front of the church. The first time she saw one of these wooden boxes, Aunt Bill didn't understand what it was for. She found out soon enough.

After the preaching, the elders opened the box and pulled out a number of poisonous snakes. As a test of faith, people came forward to handle the snakes, believing they would only be hurt by their bite if they had hidden sin in their lives. If they were pure and had strong faith they would avoid this judgment.

Despite her previous experience with snakes in the circus, Aunt Bill wanted no part of this. She hightailed it out of there like her feet were on fire and never looked back.

This emphasis on sin and judgment was typical of the churches I grew up around. It shaped an image of God that I still have to struggle with sometimes, a God who is angry and judgmental and looking for a chance to catch me in sin so that He can punish me. Consequently, I felt I had to work hard to impress Him somehow in order to get Him to overlook my mistakes.

I believed that God constantly scrutinized my actions, frowned on my folly, demanded perfection, and was disappointed in me when I offered Him anything less. Deep down, I was afraid of Him. He was not someone who loved and accepted me. He was someone who judged me, whose standards I could not live up to.

But isn't that what grace is all about? That through Jesus Christ, God accepts me as I am—a weak, wounded, and imperfect person. That if I am to change, it will have to be with His help.

I can't really say when I crossed the line from the judgmental God of my childhood to the understanding I now possess. I guess this kind of change happens slowly and over time. But the things I have read, the experiences I have had, and the quiet work of the Spirit in my heart all have led me to discover the true character of God.

A God who loves me.

A God I can trust.

While it is true that He is powerful and holy, He is also forgiving and accepting. He sees into the very depths of my soul and loves me as only a father could.

This discovery is like finding the first flower that blooms on the first day of spring—the basis for hope and the key to overcoming a life filled with fear.

Hollis

H is name was Hollis.

There were some pretty unusual people in the town where I grew up. But none fit in less well than Hollis.

It was not uncommon for us to see him whenever my family drove into town. As our car sped past, I would catch a glimpse of Hollis pushing an old green bike along the side of the road. With its flat tires and bent frame, his bike looked like the least efficient form of transportation that I could imagine. Come to think of it, I don't believe I ever actually saw him ride it. Instead, he wheeled it along the road, his hands firmly gripping the rusted handlebars, his boots stirring little eddies of dust, and his flowered dress gently being lifted by the breeze from each passing car.

Hollis lived in Cumberland Gap, Tennessee, but made the thirty-minute walk across the mountain to Middlesboro, Kentucky, several times a week. His destination was usually the dress shop located on Main Street.

It was not uncommon to see him on the sidewalk, his bike leaned up against the shop window, his face pressed against the glass, filled with longing.

There he would stand, the wind pressing the hem of his thrift store dress against his hairy, muscular legs as he peered longingly at the beautiful dresses that filled the racks of the store. He so much wanted one of the stylish new dresses that adorned the front window. Tears trickled down his cheeks, smearing his mascara as he tried to brush them away.

Hollis was either oblivious to the opinions of others or else he just didn't care anymore. He didn't seem to notice the stares and the laughter and the cruel comments. It was as if he was wearing an invisible armor that protected him from the hurtful words that people threw like stones.

We never really knew very much about Hollis; where he had come from or what had made him the way he was. We only knew that he was different.

And we knew that his heart must be filled with pain.

Perhaps after so many years of abuse he had simply retreated inside himself, like a turtle into its shell, into a safe place, a place where there was one single vision, one unfulfilled dream that drove him forward.

Hollis wanted to be a woman.

IN A PLACE LIKE MIDDLESBORO, KENTUCKY, no one knew what to do with someone like Hollis. I'm sure it comes as no surprise that he didn't meet with much acceptance. In Middlesboro, conformity was expected. In our little town even a woman who dressed just a bit different from the crowd or a man with a car just a bit more sporty than the norm would attract a great deal of attention. Heads would turn. Rumors would fly.

Can you imagine then how the local rednecks reacted to a man whose one desire in life was to be a woman?

Some mocked and ridiculed him.

Some seemed angry and threatened by him.

Some reacted in what may be an even more cruel manner. They simply acted as if he didn't exist.

But my family sought to reach out in whatever small ways we could.

Some days, when we'd spot him shuffling along the side of the road and if we had a little room to spare, Dad would pull over and offer him a ride. We'd stop and motion him to get in, Dad helping him put his beat-up bicycle into the back of our truck.

Seeing him up close helped me to look past his strange choice of clothing. His skin always seemed to be tanned and his hair was a dirty blond color. But the one thing I couldn't help notice about him were his eyes. They were a beautiful, clear green color. But there was something in his eyes that was deeper and more heartbreaking than I could fully understand at my young age. I think it was a deep sense of being alone.

Hollis was an outsider.

ONE DAY MY MOTHER AND I WERE shopping at the Woolworth store in Middlesboro. The new school year was just beginning, and I needed a nightgown and some new clothes for school.

Mom and I were browsing through the underwear table, evaluating the options that presented themselves, when I looked up to see a familiar pair of green eyes staring back at me.

Hollis.

"Hello, Lola! Hello, Cindy! How are y'all doin'?" he said in his very effeminate hillbilly accent.

Mom smiled and returned his greeting.

"You know, Lola," he offered, "you can call me Holly if you like."

I was mortified.

I tried to slip under the table before anyone noticed we were talking to him.

The conversation soon turned to the hormone pills he was taking, and while he talked he nonchalantly tried several different bras on over his shirt.

Mother seemed unfazed by this, and smiled kindly as she listened. Then she paused just a moment and said, "Hollis, why do you want to be a woman?"

Hollis began to explain that he had, from the time he was very young, always felt trapped inside the body of a stranger. He told us of his longing to be beautiful and feminine.

As she listened patiently, smiling gently at him, I could see the deep compassion my mother felt for this poor man. Though I was young and embarrassed to be seen in conversation with this strange man, I could not help but feel deep inside a sense of pride at my mother's understanding and kindness.

At the way she treated him like a real person.

At the way she seemed to sense his pain and loneliness.

Unlike nearly everyone else in town, she was not afraid of him.

Before he left us, he asked mother to pray for him. She promised she would. Then she said, very softly, but very firmly, "Hollis, remember this: No matter what, Jesus loves you."

He smiled a sad smile, said goodbye, and walked away.

I've OFTEN WONDERED WHATEVER happened to Hollis. I heard a rumor that he had died of AIDS. That seems likely. I'm pretty sure that his life was filled with a great deal of sadness, fear, and confusion. I wonder if he ever knew that he was not alone. Really understood that Jesus loved him. I wonder if he remembered the words my mother spoke to him that day in Woolworth's.

I have found that fear can keep me from reaching out to others, especially those who are a bit unusual or who make me feel uncomfortable.

I pray for courage to reach out to the Hollis' in my life, to have the strength to look past their differences and honor them as an individual. To look deeply into their eyes and see a person much beloved by God.

1970

Samuel & Me
(The only picture I have of
the two of us.)

Roho

It's probably obvious by now that I grew up in a large family. There was my natural sister, Sam, my brother Mike, my half brother Haze, and two adopted sisters, Tammy and Sherry. (Before they became our sisters, Tammy and Sherry were our first cousins.) Then there was Samuel.

Samuel holds a unique place in our family history. The stories passed down indicate that there was something special about him from the very beginning.

He was the only one of the children to inherit my father's hazel eyes, and he had a smile that was both sweet and mischievous. Behind his eyes lurked a soul that seemed too wise for his young age.

Samuel was only four when Mom and Dad discovered a lump in his lower abdomen. They had been concerned about his weight for some time and were puzzled by the fact that he was never hungry and always weak.

They took Samuel to a doctor who performed a series of tests that led to exploratory surgery. What they found was the worst news that a parent could receive.

Samuel was dying of cancer.

It was lymphoma, a rare and aggressive cancer that travels through the blood, producing massive tumors throughout the body. In the early seventies the treatment for this kind of cancer was experimental at best. The only thing for my parents to do was to pray and take their chances on the best that modern medicine could offer.

SAMUEL NEEDED TO TAKE A COURSE of medicines before he was hospitalized, but he was resistant to swallowing the unpleasant tasting pills. And it wasn't really possible to force him to take his medicine. Daddy grew desperate and soon hatched a plan.

Samuel had always loved horses, so Daddy bought him a pony that we named Cocoa.

Daddy would beg Samuel to take just a little medicine in exchange for a ride on Cocoa. Sometimes it worked. Sometimes it didn't.

Then he tried other incentives—a Big Wheel bike and various kinds of toys—items that he really couldn't afford on his meager mechanic's salary. But the best incentive came in the form of an Easter present from my Aunt Frieda: a red rooster my dad named Roho.

SAMUEL LOVED ROHO LIKE nothing else.

They would chase each other around the backyard, laughing and flapping and squawking.

Roosters have a reputation for being temperamental, and Roho was no exception. He left scars on all of us. I still have a scar on my stomach from when he spurred me when I was only three. But he never hurt Samuel.

He loved Samuel and was even protective of him.

It was almost as though that rooster could sense the pain Samuel was in.

Soon, Samuel was taken to a hospital in Oak Ridge, Tennessee. They tried countless experimental treatments, hoping that something would make a difference. This went on for months, with Mom by his bedside five days a week. Daddy had to keep working to support the family and pay the hospital bills, but would go in to relieve her on the weekends.

Many ministers were summoned to pray for Samuel's healing, including a handful of self-proclaimed faith healers who told Mom that Samuel would be healed if she just had enough faith. They made her feel that the weight of the outcome was on her weary shoulders.

They'd come and go like a revolving door at a tent revival.

Still Mama sat and prayed and waited for the healing to take place.

It never did.

Samuel and I were only a year apart in age. Although we were close playmates, to this day I only carry one clear memory of him.

He was about halfway through his treatment when one day he made a special request: he wanted to see Roho.

So we put our red rooster in our little VW and drove to the hospital. When we arrived we discovered that the chicken would not be permitted inside the hospital because of sanitary concerns.

We refused to give up easily.

We walked around the outside of the hospital and found the window to Samuel's room. It was high off the ground, so my brother Mike lifted me up on his shoulders and held me up in front of the window. I held Roho up so that Samuel could see the rooster he loved so much. Roho never squirmed or made a fuss or tried to get away.

Samuel beamed with delight.

BUT IT WOULD BE THE LAST TIME Samuel saw Roho.

After six months of treatment, Samuel grew so weak that the only way he could communicate was by blinking his eyes to say yes and no.

Only eight months after his diagnosis, Samuel gave up the fight and walked out of the hospital in the company of angels.

It was one week before his fifth birthday.

AS I FEEL MY BABY TURNING and kicking inside me, I have only an inkling of the pain my parents must have gone through and the questions they must have asked.

Why did God let this happen?

Why would those ignorant people who professed to have healing power tell my mother that Samuel's healing was dependent upon her faith?

Why, with all the murderers, rapists, and drug addicts walking around fat and healthy, would God choose to take an innocent and curious little boy?

I have no answers to these questions, only frustration. But my husband recently said something that helps me grasp a little of the mystery.

Our baby, he said, is surely very happy right now, safe and warm and protected in the womb. She would probably be content to stay right there forever. She will not enjoy the difficult journey that lies ahead as she forges her way into this world. And yet God has this beautiful place waiting for her when she arrives to be with us. But our baby can't see what's waiting for her, so she would probably be happy to remain in the womb, where she is comfortable and secure.

But think what she'd be missing!

Samuel's journey, though very brief, held the pain of a lifetime. But he walked through that pain into a new place, a place where Jesus was waiting to love him and hold him and show him a world that he had only seen in dreams.

He passed through the pain and found a world better than this one.

As for Roho, he went on to be with Samuel a short time later. I know that some people will dispute the idea that animals and humans will share the same heaven, but I believe that right now Roho and Samuel are laughing and chasing each other around some eternal golden meadow— happy, free, and together again.

Samuel and Robo

Rejection

Doug Barnard.

I'll never forget the day he first walked into my seventh-grade class. He had blond hair, sparkling green eyes, and a splash of freckles across his perfect nose. It was as if I could hear music in his footsteps and a song in his voice.

I fell hopelessly in love.

The unfortunate thing for me was that I was shy, a bit chubby, and definitely not one of the "hip" chicks in our class.

What made the situation even more hopeless was that every other girl, including the prissy cheerleaders and the well-toned and athletic girls of the basketball team, felt the same way about Doug as I did.

But I did not give up.

Sometimes I would work up the nerve to smile and say hello to him when we passed in the hall or when we ended up at the water fountain at the same time. He would respond with a quick "hi" and then dart off.

As the year progressed, I went in for more drastic tactics, such as offering him the cookies and chocolate milk from my lunch tray. His muttered response was invariable: "Yeah, sure. Thanks."

I never did tell him how I felt about him. I guess I was afraid he'd laugh at me. My lips remained silent while my offerings of cookies and milk continued. I hoped that one day he might see the light.

I'll never know what he might have said if I'd ever had the nerve to confess my feelings...

OF COURSE I NO LONGER PINE after Doug Barnard, but the tendencies I learned from how I related to him have stuck with me. The fear of rejection has followed me throughout my life. It has made me silent when I had something to say. It was often my version of hiding my lamp under a bushel.

In my early years of performing live music, I was very apprehensive about playing with musicians who were more advanced and sophisticated on their instruments than I was. After all, my approach to the piano is probably about 90 percent instinct and emotion and about 10 percent technical ability.

But many times, I did have something worth sharing. I was, however, afraid to voice new ideas for fear they would be rejected or quietly ignored and forgotten.

In time I learned the foolishness of this attitude. Most musicians are always open to new ideas. It is part of what makes playing live music so interesting.

The problem was in my head.

But the fear of being rejected, of not being taken seriously, is not an easy fear to overcome.

I'M LEARNING THAT THE ONLY WAY to grow, whether it be in musical ability or in personality and character, is to take some risks.

Sure, sometimes a bad idea will need to be thrown out and it is true that some "rabbit trails" lead to dead ends, but that is no excuse to give up.

We must learn to have faith in the way that God is working within us. We must learn to take some risks.

If we don't, we'll just continue to revolve in a world of stifling sameness.

We'll never catch the new vision, the one that waits just around the bend.

But if we face our fear of being rejected, and find the courage that comes from knowing God accepts us, we can break through the veil and see the world in the startling beauty of newness.

First Band

Tony Miracle, Brent Barcus & Brent Leithall

Finding My Song

One of the most common questions people ask me is: "How did you get your start in music?"

For me, it all began on the bench of an old mahogany grand piano that my grandfather had restored. I was about nine years old when my love affair with the piano and poetry began.

I would sit for hours, plunking out the notes to songs I'd heard on television or the radio, trying to figure them out for myself. I attempted to take a couple of piano lessons but didn't have much success, so I abandoned them pretty quickly. I didn't learn to master the technical ins and outs of the keyboard, but I loved the mystery of sitting down to the piano and discovering something new that would reflect my sadness or my joy.

The first piece I learned to play was Henry Mancini's theme to *The Pink Panther*. Then I graduated to a classic piece, Beethoven's "Moonlight Sonata," which still remains one of my favorites.

WHEN WE MOVED TO THE CABIN in the hollow we left the mahogany piano in storage and replaced it with an old black upright. It had seen better days, its keys now yellowed by the years, but it still had a sweet sound and I loved to play it.

I was never very active in sports or social activities at school.

I tried out for the basketball team, but I didn't make it.

I tried out for the drill team, but I didn't make it.

Although I became a little discouraged by these failures, my lack of extracurricular activities left me with plenty of time to practice on the piano. And I not only practiced, but I also wrote songs.

I would meander down the sandy road that ran alongside the river, stopping to sit on the bank and reflect on life and nature and the God who created them. I'd daydream and write poetry and then bring those thoughts to the helm of that old black upright piano. That's where the songwriter in me was born.

Music became my way of contributing to the world, of leaving my mark.

I never passed up an opportunity to play or sing. I performed the National Anthem at football games, and sang for pageants, plays, and chapel services.

Though I was painfully shy, my desire to share music with others was greater than my shyness.

It took a while for me to able to make a career of music. My first job was as a fountain girl and sometime skater at the Sonic Drive-In, then I spent a couple years substitute teaching. My teaching career ended on the day when a boy in my sixth-grade class intentionally threw up just to gross everybody out (a trick he'd pulled with other teachers). When I held firm in discipline and told him to get the supplies from the janitor to clean up his mess, he told me he was "gonna have his mom beat me up." I decided that substitute teaching wasn't for me. After that, I worked my way up to assistant manager at Claire's Boutique while keeping a second job at a dress shop that was just across from Claire's in the mall.

But all this time, what I really wanted to do was sing and write songs.

ONE DAY MY FRIEND JIMMY BRYANT coerced me into entering a talent contest at a place called Dollywood, a sort of amusement park named for Dolly Parton. I told him I didn't want to enter because cloggers always seem to win these kinds of contests, but I entered anyway. To my surprise, I won.

Part of the prize was a contract to perform at Dollywood, which I did for two seasons. During the off-season I met a man named Norbert Stovall, who owned a recording studio in Knoxville, Tennessee, called "Big Mama's" (a nickname everyone called his mother, who was at best four and a half feet tall and weighed a little over 90 pounds). Norbert hired me to do some background vocals and then gave me a full-time job helping to run the office and doing secretarial work (which I was terrible at!). In the evenings I'd set aside the typewriter and would sing lead or backing vocals on a series of albums called *You Sing the Hits*. Though I was only paid $10 per song, the experience I gained was priceless. I worked 14-hour days six days a week, but I loved it.

But after three years of this pace my voice was tired and I was weary of trying to sound like other people. I took a break and worked for a while at a men's clothing store, but still kept my hand in music by being part of a show that performed on Tuesday and Thursday nights in Gatlinburg, Tennessee.

The show was held over top of a chicken restaurant. The music and humor was like the *Hee Haw* show on a really bad night. It was 100 percent cheese and I hated it. But it led to some good connections.

Kirk Talley, a talented singer/songwriter and a member of the southern gospel group, The Talleys, had gotten me the job with a men's clothing store and also helped me make a connection with someone from Star Search. I did a simple demo of four songs to send them. Without telling me, Kirk also sent the demo to John Mays, an A & R (Artist and Repertoire) Director at Word Records.

John liked what he heard, so Kirk and I drove to Nashville to meet with him. I felt pretty stressed about the meeting, but as soon as I met John I knew there was nothing to worry about. He was one of the nicest people I ever met. Over a lunch at a local Mexican restaurant we decided that we'd cut a couple of demos, see how they sounded, and then take it from there.

So, for the next several months I spent my day off driving to Nashville to work with John and with Mark Hammond, a hot young producer in Nashville. These demos led to an album deal with Word Records.

ALL THOSE YEARS SITTING AT THE piano writing songs had led to this. And I am grateful to God for all the wonderful people who helped and encouraged me along the way. It still amazes me to think that the shy young girl at the piano now performs every year before many thousands of people.

God moves in mysterious ways.

Roses were sent to celebrate my first # 1 Song "Let it Be Lone"

Recording Session for "Under the Waterfall"
David Huff, Ronnie Brookshire, Tommy Sims,
Mark Hammond and Dave Dilbeck

We Fall Down

One of the unfortunate parts of being a performer is that when you make a mistake, you often get to make it in front of a big crowd of people.

Thankfully, two of my most embarrassing moments came pretty early in my singing career. Maybe I've worked most of the bugs out. Of course, one never knows what the future might hold!

BEFORE I RECORDED MY FIRST RECORD, I was working as a waitress at West End Cooker and doing background vocal work to earn extra money. I was lucky enough to snag a job doing several weekend concerts performing backup vocals for a wonderful singer named David Miller.

Early one Saturday morning I left town with a friend and fellow vocalist, Nicole Coleman, to back up David, who was appearing in Memphis, Tennessee, at the Beale Street Festival. Although I had grown up in Tennessee, I'd never been to Memphis.

I fell in love with the city, its sights and smells and sounds.

We had a few hours before the concert, so I joined several of the musicians in exploring famous Beale Street. We found ourselves jostled along the crowded sidewalks in the ninety-eight degree sunshine.

It was hot and humid when we set out, but as the evening approached a gentle southern breeze came off the river.

Blues music drifted out from nearly every open door, along with the smell of barbecue and funnel cakes.

The air felt warm and golden as the day settled down into a southern summer night. It seemed like perfect weather for rocking chairs, front porches, and slices of cold watermelon.

By the time we were to perform, the schedule had already fallen hopelessly behind. All day long the stage had been filled with a full roster of performers, one after the other. We weren't sure how soon we'd be on.

I came out of the bathroom, gave myself one final fluff and spray, and joined the guys in David's horn section who were hanging around in the front lounge area. I was enjoying the conversation, but kept glancing at my watch, realizing that the starting time for David's performance had already passed, and we still had not yet done our sound check.

Suddenly, ringing over the sound system, I heard the first notes of David's first song. Had they started the sound check, I wondered?

Running to the door, I saw that they had dispensed with the sound check and launched right into the first song.

I ran from the trailer to the steps of the stage, clearly visible to the listening audience. Attempting to climb the steps as quickly as possible, I managed to get my pants snagged in the wooden steps. In no time at all, the sheer Palatso pants I was wearing were down around my knees in full view of the crowd.

It was quite an entrance.

And I was mortified.

I sat down, twisted around, and got my pants back on before joining the other background singers on their platform.

I was red-faced and humiliated.

The rest of the band got a pretty good laugh out of my embarrassment.

Later I learned that the horn section didn't play until the second half of the show, so that's why they had been in no hurry.

OF COURSE, VARIOUS OTHER THINGS have left me feeling embarrassed.

Still being busy in the bathroom when the master of ceremonies introduced me (and wearing a headset microphone that I prayed was not turned on!).

Forgetting the words to my own songs. Going completely blank.

Then there was the night I closed with an enthusiastic, "Good night, Toledo. We love you!" only to have someone in the front row point out that we were in Rockford, Illinois.

BUT THE OTHER MOMENT OF greatest mortification came during Steven Curtis Chapman's "Great Adventure Tour." Susan Ashton and Out of the Grey joined me on this tour with Steven, but I was the new young artist. My record had only been out a short time.

Susan got very sick one night, so I filled in for her.

I was incredibly nervous anyway, but I was such an admirer of Steven's music that I felt a lot of pressure to make a good impression.

At this point in my career, I did a lot of dancing as part of my performance, energetically running from one end of the stage to the other. That night I even put tape on the bottom of my new pair of shoes to give me a little extra traction.

It wasn't quite enough.

During the song "It's Gonna Be Heaven," everything was going well when suddenly my foot lost traction, and I slipped on the slick stage floor.

Down I went.

Hard.

There was a collective gasp from the audience as I lay there stunned for a moment.

Finally, I got up and finished. Embarrassed, but glad I wasn't seriously hurt.

And though I thought that Steven hadn't noticed my fall, he brought it up six years later when we shared the stage at a Gospel Music Association songwriter's showcase. In the middle of our onstage banter, he told the whole story.

He laughed.

The audience laughed.

And so did I.

I'VE LEARNED THAT I CANNOT take myself too seriously. I need to be able to laugh at my own follies and failures, and not be afraid to let people see that I make mistakes.

It can be comforting when we realize that our imperfections are what endear us to others. I've always struggled with the tendency to be a perfectionist, but I'm learning that life itself is a pretty imperfect thing sometimes.

Only God is perfect. I'm not. And that's ok.

Realizing that takes away some of the pressure.

It's ok to fall down sometimes. As long as we always get back up.

Video Shoot for "I'll Stand"

How Did I Get Here?

I t is fall 1995.

In the wee hours of the morning the alarm sounds insistently in my ear. Rolling over, I force my eyes open to read the time: 3:30 A.M.

It has only been two and a half hours since I crawled exhausted into bed. The concert went late and by the time I got myself checked into the hotel room it was already 1:00 A.M.

I lie here trying to summon the energy needed to throw my feet over the side of the bed. My eyes open very reluctantly, slowly, like a rusty screen door. It is still dark outside, the only illumination in my room coming from glowing red numerals on the clock. They are telling me to get up.

I want to sleep.

I want to forget about how this dream turned into such a nightmare: three years of nonstop traveling, very little sleep, the constant pressure of performing, and the most recent addition to my stress—nodules on my vocal cords, a medical condition brought on by using my voice too much and in the wrong way. And the lack of sleep makes it worse.

So this is the glamorous life of a recording artist on tour...

EVERY CONCERT I FIND MYSELF wondering if I will make it through the night.

Without panic, without losing my voice, without collapsing in sheer exhaustion.

I swing my legs over the edge of the bed and force myself to get up. My movements are like those of a robot in need of a good tune-up.

Somehow I manage to get myself ready and I meet the band in the lobby. We are off to the airport and arrive in Denver a few hours later for a morning concert.

I feel more exhausted than I ever have in my life. It feels like I am coming down with bronchitis again, which means I'll need to go see my doctor, who will give me another steroid shot that will magically give me back my voice for a couple of days. Then the bottom will drop out again and I'll feel even worse. Hopefully this time I'll be sick during one of the rare stretches when there are no concerts scheduled.

NOW I'M HOLDING A NEW HOTEL room key in my hand and have less than an hour to get myself ready. I open the door, throw my luggage on the bed, and dig out my makeup bag.

The room is beautiful and the bathroom is especially nice. Marble everywhere. Gold faucets. A big tub, which calls me to a luxurious bubble bath. But there is no time for that.

As I run the brush through my hair, I gaze into the mirror. I don't like the look of the person who stares back at me. Her eyes are red and swollen. Her skin is dry. Her hair is limp and unmanageable. She looks tired. And sad.

I peer more intently into the mirror, as though I'm looking for a place to escape. Now I see another girl looking back at me...

IT WAS MY FIRST PHOTO SHOOT. I had just spent three hours in the hair and makeup chair with a man who spoke with the lilt of a French girl and told me stories of doing the hair of supermodels like Cindy Crawford and Naomi Campbell.

Here I was. A young girl, still wet behind the ears, from a little valley called "Snake Holler."

My world was certainly changing.

I excused myself to go to the bathroom and climbed down out of the chair. As I stepped into the bathroom I got my first glimpse of my new look in the mirror. I was stunned. I felt both joy at the results of the hairdresser's efforts and fear, knowing that there was no way I could possibly duplicate this look in my everyday life.

THIS WAS CLEARLY NOT THE SAME girl who stared back at me now. Grasping for my makeup brush, I try to paint life onto my face. But it is no use. I pull my hair into a ponytail and wonder how I got here.

Whatever possessed me to embrace such a life?

I drop my brush and grab hold of the edge of the sink to retain my balance. I crumple and fold, sinking onto the floor as hot tears drop down onto cold marble.

"God," I cry, "please help me. I cannot go on like this..."

I CAN ALMOST HEAR THE MUSIC from that old upright piano.

The heavy oak door is open to our log cabin, and the screen door is all that separates us from the yawning beagle lying on the front porch with his nose to the screen, sniffing the aroma of dinner wafting out into the humid air along with the melancholy music I am making.

My dad is lying on the couch listening to me play over the hum of a large window box fan. Mama is frying chicken and potatoes.

Outside the colors of summer have mellowed into the bouquet of fall. Leaves are perched high on their branches, their reds and oranges and golds waving in the sunlight before they surrender and drift toward the ground.

I am the only child still at home. All my brothers and sisters have already left the nest. I am struggling through the seventh grade and consumed with literature, poetry, and music. Most days I take long walks in my bare feet down the sandy road that leads to the creek.

Our house sits in a valley that local legend says was formed by a meteor many moons ago. The trees which circle in close about the house make us feel like we are in some great nest and that the hand of God feeds and watches over us.

On starry nights I stare into the great circle above and dream of seeing all that awaits me in my life.

I will travel. I will unlock the mysteries of love and life.

I am convinced that the way to find the answers is in the music that falls from heaven into my heart. I write down everything I feel. I pray that God will show me the way to use my love of music.

As THE OLD SAYING GOES, "Be careful what you pray for. You might get it."

I open my eyes and am pulled back into my current dismal reality.

Here is what dawns on me like a winter morning: There is no longer any joy in my song.

My song is one of fear and anxiety.

The fear of the next note cracking in my throat. The fear of what people will think. The fear of failing.

I remember the words my mother used to quote and they ring in my ear: "God has not given us a spirit of fear, but of power and of love and of a sound mind."

I pray anew that God will be with me in this journey I am traveling. I see that the footprints belong to me.

A prayer is sent up and a seed is planted.

One step in the right direction. Miles still left to go.

But a glimmer of hope beckons me out of my valley of despair.

Listen Tour

Sketches from the Road

It occurs to me that I have written so much about the difficulties that have come out of my years of touring. I fear I have painted a picture that focuses only on the hard times, neglecting the many wonderful moments and experiences.

But I want you to know that I am so very grateful to be able to make a living doing what I love to do. Music and writing are as much a part of me as my arms and legs. Nothing could take the place of music in my life. I wouldn't even want to imagine what life would be like without it and without the opportunity to share my gifts with others.

Along with the heartaches and disappointments have come many magical moments, experiences that I will always remember.

Moments and memories…

I WAS PERFORMING IN Virginia Beach, Virginia in the conference center owned by the 700 Club. It was one of those "bare bones" performances that I love to do so much, just me and one band member, Drew. No elaborate accompaniment. Just an acoustic guitar, a piano, and a little percussion.

We got there early to do a sound check, and as we passed through the hotel we were introduced to a sweet young man named William.

His skin was the color of chocolate and his beautiful smile seemed to light up his whole face.

He was polite, sharp, and very witty; a joy to talk with, though his speech was halting and slow. William had to live with multiple sclerosis.

Though his body was challenged by this disease, his spirit was free and unbridled. He reminded me a little of the man named Wimpy who ran the local country store near where I grew up. I remember visiting Wimpy's store almost every day and watching as he slowly and painstakingly tapped out our purchase on an old manual cash register, trying to control his hand by grasping it firmly with the other one. His speech was slow and labored, but he was unfailingly kind and—if you listened patiently—very intelligent. I remember Daddy saying that he was no different from anybody else, that we should not judge him less able or treat him differently. Trapped inside a body with multiple sclerosis were a keen mind and the kindest of hearts. He was in a prison not of his own making. That is what William struggled with as well.

After talking with him for a few moments, we ambled over to the auditorium for a sound check.

The concert that night was a lot of fun. It got off to a shaky start, however, when they introduced me and I wasn't there. Needless to say, this caused a little confusion. At that moment I was in a restroom that was quite a long way from the stage.

So, when I finally made it to the piano bench, I told the audience where I'd been and we all laughed together. The warmth that evening was amazing. I felt a real connection with the audience.

When I came to the closing song, "I Will Be Free," I asked the audience to sing it with me.

> *I will be free*
> *I will be free to run the mountains*
> *I will be free*
> *Free to drink from the living fountain*
> *Oh, I'll never turn back 'cause He waits for me*
> *Oh I will be free.*

As we sang, a voice floated up from the crowd, a voice like an angel.

It did not stand out because of its beauty, but because of its brokenness. It was the brokenness of a hungry and willing heart singing praise to God.

When I followed the voice, it led me to a pair of brown eyes brimming with tears. And a glorious smile.

It was William.

I felt as though I had no control over what happened next. I looked at him, got up from the piano, and motioned for him to come forward. He came, moving with an awkward and determined gait.

I stood there beside him as he slid onto the piano bench. I had no idea that he played the piano. In fact, I didn't even know why I had asked him to come forward.

Neither did he. But he came.

He started to sing and play. And it was as if heaven itself had opened up its floodgates to let the fountain of living water shower down upon us. The feeling in the room was something beyond this world.

People were crying and laughing. Drew and I stood there frozen, barely able to breathe, drinking in the moment, that little glimpse of heaven.

What we saw was this: In that moment we glimpsed how beautiful William was and saw that the shackles that constrained his body and voice had, for that moment, come undone. As a result, so had ours.

It was a taste of freedom and a glimpse of eternity, when we will all be healed and made whole.

✦ ✦ ✦ ✦ ✦

ONE OF THE MOST INTIMATE CONCERTS I ever played was in Kissimmee, Florida, at a county fair. As our van neared the stage, there—front and center—was an audience of one.

One person.

My road manager and I looked at each other and didn't know whether to laugh or cry.

To top things off, the stage was the hollowed out side of a barn and my dressing room was a horse stall. But there was a saving grace: a lovely, large grand piano in the center of the stage. Oh well, the show must go on…

As the time drew near for the show to begin, we looked out from my stall to see that a few more people had joined the one lonely concertgoer. It was to be a "concert under the stars," so everyone was spreading out their blankets and getting comfy, settling in for an evening of music.

It wasn't a huge crowd, but they were very appreciative. It was a beautiful evening. Until…

I was about halfway through my set list when I noticed that people were looking warily up at the sky, which was filling up with dark clouds.

And then it all happened so fast.

A clap of thunder echoed in the distance, followed by a flash of lightning.

My road manager ran over to me and took the cordless microphone out of my hands for fear of electric shock.

Then the sky opened up and it began to pour.

Not just a gentle rain, but sheets of hard, driving rain.

Without really thinking, I yelled out and motioned the audience to join me on the platform. The entire audience rushed up the stairs and onto the stage. There we all were, huddled together under the safety of the barn, listening to the rain hit the tin roof.

So we gathered around the piano and sang old hymns together.

One after the other, we sang some of the classic songs of faith.

And as the final notes of "Amazing Grace" lingered in the air, the rain suddenly stopped.

We all left the stage together that night, knowing that we had shared something magical. In the midst of a storm, we had all found shelter under an old barn and in the arms of God.

✦ ✦ ✦ ✦ ✦

I'VE LEARNED THAT SOMETIMES GOD uses us in ways we never would have expected. In fact, sometimes you feel sort of insignificant in the bigger scheme of what God is up to.

The tour to promote the album, *Listen*, was a grueling one. We traveled by bus from city to city, usually sleeping as the driver shuttled us to the next place on our itinerary. Toward the end of the tour, we caught a flight out to California to do a series of five concerts with Phil and Betty, two of the sweetest concert promoters you'd ever want to meet.

Our first performance was in Fresno. Since we had flown, my stage clothes—which usually would have been hanging up in the bus—were a mess, crumpled and wrinkled from being packed in my suitcase. Since I had left my steamer behind on the bus, I didn't know quite what to do.

Reluctantly, I asked one of the concert staff if they had an iron. Figuring that it was unlikely that there would be one in the building, they sent someone out to find an iron for me.

After sound check, I went back to my dressing room and found an iron waiting. I pressed my clothes and got myself ready.

It was only after the show that I heard what had happened.

The promoters had sent one of the concert volunteers to get an iron from the home of one of the church members. Since that person wasn't home, they were given a key and directions for where the iron was kept. The volunteer used the key to let themselves in and made their way upstairs. When they reached the top of the stairs they discovered the teenage daughter of the church member sitting on her bed with a gun to her head. She was about to commit suicide.

The volunteer, though shocked at her discovery, calmly talked with the young girl and convinced her to put down the gun and get some help.

A potential suicide was averted by my need for an iron. God moves in some pretty mysterious ways.

Whenever I find myself wishing that He would make Himself more clearly known, I remember moments like this and recognize that His wise hand is always at work in our lives.

God builds a bridge to the broken.

Sometimes He creates a wrinkle in time.

✦ ✦ ✦ ✦ ✦

IF THERE IS A SONG THAT I FEEL defines me as a person and an artist, it would have to be "I Will Be Free." Over the years I have received hundreds of letters referring to it and had numerous conversations with people who were encouraged by the song during a difficult time in their lives.

Of the many special moments connected with this song, there is one that stands alone.

I can't remember what city we were in or the name of the church, but everything else comes back to me clearly.

I can see the padded pews, the carpeted stage, the piano.

I was still trying to recover my voice and was in the midst of intense vocal lessons, aimed at healing and rebuilding my damaged vocal chords.

Unfortunately, on that night, in the battle between fear and me, I was losing ground. I found myself completely focused on every note I sang. Instead of just letting the songs flow out of me, I was worried about how it sounded, about what the audience was hearing.

The battle was spiritual as much as it was physical.

At the end of the evening I came to the most vocally demanding song of the night, the song I would close with: "I Will Be Free."

How ironic that a song that spoke of having freedom in God was the ball and chain that wrapped around my voice.

Just before I started to sing, knowing it would probably be a terrible performance, I decided to confess to the audience where I was at and what I was going through. I shared with them the troubles I was experiencing with my voice and noted that this night had been especially difficult. But if they were willing to listen, I'd risk embarrassment and sing one last song, the most challenging one to sing.

So I began. The notes scraped against my throat on the verse and when it came to the chorus my voice just stopped.

There was nothing left, but the melody did not die.

The audience began to sing.

They sang to me because I couldn't sing to them.

I sat there and accompanied them on the piano as they sang the words and it all washed over me. They carried me when I could not walk any further. They soothed my soul.

My tears fell freely, streaming down my face and onto the ivory keys.

That night a room full of angels sang to a wounded heart and gave me a new song to sing.

And I was free.

Honey, Betsy,
and an Autumn Day

The fear of losing someone you love deeply is a fear that is, I guess, very real to most of us.

You fear that the phone will ring in the middle of the night and the message you hear will knock the wind out of you. You know that a part of you will be lost in losing one you love so very much.

Sitting in the safety of a hotel room following a concert, I'll sometimes hear the insistent shrill whine of a siren building, then fading as an ambulance rushes by. When I hear this sound, I say a prayer for whoever is facing tragedy at that moment. And for those who love them.

And I pray a prayer of thanks that it isn't me.

ABOUT A YEAR AGO, it was me.

I was awakened on a sunny Friday morning with the news that my father had, suddenly and unexpectedly, died during the night, the victim of a massive coronary.

At first, I simply didn't know what to do.

It felt as though the world had stopped and the only true reality was my own tragic fate: I had lost something unspeakably precious. I knew my world would never be the same again, just as it was not the same for friends who had lost parents, spouses, brothers and sisters. I can recall how sad I felt for them. But it is impossible to know how utterly empty life feels at a time like this until death touches you personally, touches parts of you that you never knew existed. What you only feared and tried not to think about has become a reality.

ONLY A FEW MONTHS EARLIER, I was visiting my parents' home in Kentucky during a beautiful autumn weekend. My mom was out of town, so it was just my dad and me.

On Saturday morning, Dad and I decided to venture out to the local flea market in nearby London, Kentucky.

The place was packed with men rummaging through old rusty car parts and tools.

Their wives were looking for antique dishes, knick-knacks, and odd little collectibles to adorn their homes.

The children who shuffled about looked bored, obviously wondering how much longer they would have to suffer through their parents' search for some sort of discarded treasure.

We wandered happily through the crowds, past rickety tables filled with hubcaps, antique radios, and old salt and pepper sets. When Dad felt the call of nature and went in search of a restroom, I strolled down a nearby aisle where I saw a hand-lettered sign that said: "Puppies for Sale."

I've always loved dogs, especially puppies. Underneath the sign was a litter of the cutest little basset hounds you've ever seen. They were adorable.

When Dad found me, I was still oohing and ahhing over the little puppies. He knelt down by me and agreed that they were cute. I said that we definitely needed to take one home with us. Boomer, a small Pomeranian that Dad had owned for many years had died recently, and I thought it would be wonderful to get a new dog to fill the void his passing had left in my parents' life. Dad was not so easily convinced, but he said we could think it over. For the moment, however, he said we needed to go elsewhere to find a restroom, for the one in the flea market was out of order.

We climbed in the truck and made our away across the road to a convenience store. I waited outside while Dad went in.

Suddenly, out of the corner of my eye I saw a small ginger-colored dog, about six inches tall and ten inches long, trotting along the sidewalk and into the parking lot. With her was a tiny version of herself, tagging along behind, small enough that it would fit in the palm of your hand. Obviously, it was a mama dog and her baby.

I leapt out of the truck and ran over to see them. The two dogs responded by jumping up on me as though I was an old and trusted friend. I petted them and scratched them behind the ears. They looked at me with moist and gentle eyes.

Just then Dad emerged from the store, shaking his head and laughing. He'd seen the dogs in the distance when we'd pulled in. "I knew you were gonna' see those dogs," he said, smiling.

A local guy walked up to us, eyeing the dogs and the way I was reacting to them. He was one of those old guys who spends a lot of time hanging around the local service station or the grocery store, wherever he can find an audience for his stories. His drawl gave away the fact that he had been born and raised in Kentucky. He gave a kind of half-smile, letting a brown dribble of chewing tobacco escape from the corner of his mouth as he spoke to us, forming his words around the great big wad of tobacco that filled one of his cheeks, "Em dawgs don't blong ta no one. That littl'un 'bout got runned over. You ort to take 'em home."

Of course I was all for it, but Dad hesitated. Maybe they did belong to someone, he suggested. It wouldn't be right to go home with someone else's dog.

I took charge of the situation.

Leaving Dad to guard the mama dog, I scooped up the puppy in my arms and went inside to ask some questions. Sure enough, the lady working inside told the same story as the man outside. In fact, she added some details to the account. It seems that she had seen the owner leave the store, get in his car, toss some dog food out the window, and drive away.

In my mind that settled it.

We drove away with the two dogs, laughing and excited by the fact that we had adopted these two enchanting little creatures. (Though Daddy still called it a "dog-napping.") Little brown eyes just stared up at us, probably wondering where we were taking them.

On the way home we gave them names. I named the little one Honey because she was so very sweet and her coat was the exact color of strained honey. Daddy named the mama Betsy—for no particular reason, as far as I know.

We gave them a home and they gave us their love.

I'M NOT SURE WHY I WANTED to tell this story. Maybe because the day we adopted Honey and Betsy was one of the last days I spent with my dad. The great rescue was the last important thing we did together. Thinking about this good and happy time is one of the ways I have dealt with the pain of losing him.

NOW MY HUSBAND AND I LIVE in Canada, and as I write this we are awaiting the birth of our first child. Honey and Betsy were left in Kentucky in the care of my sister and her kids. Occasionally I miss those two little dogs and wish I had them here with me to remind me of my dad. I fear that the memories of him will one day slip away from me— I want to hold on tightly to every picture and thought.

Perhaps I'll bring Honey and Betsy home to Canada some day so I can have them near. I want to watch them play and run free until they are each very old. Then, when the time comes, I will bury them high on a hill in Canada and plant wildflowers around their graves.

THERE ARE MEMORIES THAT LIVE IN our hearts that will be with us until the time we all go home. Home to a safer and better place.

A place where we will be united with those we have loved once again.

Daddy and I in Knoxville, Tn. the
night Sigmund and I got engaged.

Breathing Again

How can I paint a picture that lets you know how bad my battle with fear eventually became? Perhaps the only way is to share a couple of entries from the journals I kept during this very dark time in my life:

> *I am lying on the couch and have just broken off a tumultuous relationship. I have come face-to-face with the pathetic state of my life. I feel paralyzed and haven't slept in days. I cannot eat. I have thrown up so much that there is nothing left but the poison in the bottom of my stomach.*
>
> *I want to go to the hospital and let them stick an IV in me so that I can finally sleep—a deep sleep where the demons cannot reach me.*
>
> *It is so hard to keep fighting. I just want to sleep.*
>
> *I lie awake and read Psalm 91 aloud. This keeps the demons away.*

Friends have stopped by to check on me and know that something is wrong. But I can't explain it. I can't speak it into the air for fear it will become stronger.

I want it to be over.

God, where is the sin in my life that has caused You to send me this nightmare? How can I pay for my sins?

I will never sin again. I will stay on this couch and read my Bible night and day if only You will take this fear from me. I will not laugh again or watch TV or do anything that takes my mind from You. Maybe then I will be strong enough to fight.

I don't know if I can fight another day.

I want to give up.

Help me not to give up.

And this:

I can see that it is a beautiful fall day outside, but I have been paralyzed for over a week, not able to go outside, to eat, to join the rest of the world.

Drew, who plays guitar with me, just called. I have canceled the concert at Café Milano. I am terrified of facing an audience, of opening my mouth. I am afraid of the monster who is just waiting to show his ugly face and take my voice away from me again.

*I am most afraid because I don't know if I'll ever
be able to get off this couch.*

I haven't eaten for several days. I feel so weak.

Drew said on the phone that he was coming by. What
will I tell him? How can I explain the craziness that is going
on inside my head?

A FEW HOURS AFTER I WROTE these words, Drew's little yellowish green Mustang pulled up in front of my house.
When I opened the door he said, "Come on outside, it's a
beautiful day!"

I stepped out on the front porch, my lungs grateful for
the blast of fresh air.

We sat on the step and he asked me what was wrong. I
wasn't even sure how to explain it. But Drew is both wise
and patient. I knew he would see past any baloney I tried
to offer him, but I was afraid to speak the truth. I knew that
I needed to do it anyway and the words tumbled out.

"I'm afraid of letting people down. I'm afraid of making
mistakes. I'm afraid of letting God down."

He listened calmly as I tried to help him understand
what I was feeling inside; all the fear that was consuming me.

When I finished, he said these words to me very gently:
"Cindy, you can't give up. You can't just stay on your couch
and read your Bible to keep from sinning. God has given
you a life to live, and you just have to do the best you can.
If you mess up and make a mistake, He'll forgive you. But
you can't stop living. You can't stop trying."

I sat silently for a moment, then felt a rush of peace come over me. He was right.

It was as if I could breathe again.

DREW CONVINCED ME TO GO AHEAD and do the concert at Café Milano. It would be, Drew said, the perfect opportunity for God to show His faithfulness. If I could muster the courage to face my fears, God would be there to give me strength.

We called the owner right then and there. I think Drew was afraid I would chicken out if I didn't commit myself to it right away.

After he left, I was still afraid, still scared to make a move. But I had begun to find strength in beginning to understand that maybe the fear I felt wasn't from God. That maybe God wanted a different life for me.

A life where I would actually enjoy singing and music and friends without feeling guilty about it.

I started eating Jell-O and bananas, slowly regaining my strength.

THE CONCERT WAS A wonderful experience.

It was the beginning of my journey back to the land of the living.

It would be a long journey, but Drew's wisdom and care had set me on the road to rediscovering how much God loved me. And that He would be there for me.

Every journey begins with a first step.

Steps Out of the Darkness

In an earlier chapter I recounted my lowest point, when I lay in a heap of tears on the bathroom floor in a hotel room. I knew then that I needed to make some major changes in my life.

There were problems to address, both internal and external.

One of the first things I had to face was my obsession with outward beauty. What I did to combat it was pretty radical, and perhaps a little crazy.

I covered every mirror in my house. The only mirror I used was the small one in my compact.

Why? Because I had become consumed by worry about my physical appearance. The fear of not looking good enough constantly haunted me.

I also covered up my television set. The only TV I watched was Charles Stanley. I found that television supplied me with an endless supply of negative information and models for beauty that were unrealistic.

It was time to purge myself of some of the lies that had created a bondage for me.

And I began to get involved in doing volunteer work, which was a wonderful way of getting my attention off me and my problems. I did this at the advice of a good friend, who thought it would do wonders for not only my soul but also for my perspective on life to do something that I would receive no praise for. Put more simply, the gift would come from giving. This was a new concept for me, because at that time, to do a concert in a church in front of other Christians offered many rewards and few sacrifices in terms of praise.

I realized that I had developed feelings of spiritual superiority as a result of beginning to believe all the wonderful things people were saying about me. I needed to be humbled and to get my priorities in order.

I also decided to start going to a counselor. It can be hard to admit you've got a problem (especially when everyone else thinks you are doing great), but this was a very good step for me. I could begin to work through my feelings, my questions, my misconceptions about God and myself.

My counselor gave me a wonderful book to read by Jerry Bridges called *Grace: It's Not Just for Beginners* that opened my eyes to understanding God's grace. I saw that a trust in God's mercy and grace had been absent from my life.

ONE OF THE MAJOR THINGS that helped me to deal with my fears was a sermon from my pastor in Knoxville, Gerald McGinnis. I listened to the tape of his sermon over and over, until I finally wore the tape out. His words were biblical, realistic, and inspiring. They were a lifeline of wisdom and hope.

Armed with these powerful thoughts and the insights from Bridges' book, I felt ready to reach for a new level of trusting God.

I was like a baby beginning anew.

Learning new things.

Relearning how to interpret my thoughts and feelings.

Allowing God to love me. And learning to love myself.

God So Loves the World

New Year's Eve.

I was in Colorado, preparing for an evening concert. I arrived exhausted at the hotel where I was staying. My room was gorgeous: luxurious thick carpeting, crown molding, high ceilings, and expensive cherry-wood furniture. Most people would have been overjoyed to get to stay in such a beautiful room.

But not me.

I'd seen too many hotel rooms and was weary from my continuing battles on the journey out of fear and into the love of God. I felt it would be unspiritual to enjoy it too much.

I closed the door behind me, dropped my bag on the bed, and took the towels off the rack to cover the mirrors and the television set.

My life was beginning to feel more manageable due to the changes that were taking place within, but my stomach still churned with doubts and confusion, with questions still unanswered.

THE ENEMY OF OUR SOULS WILL use any method he can to
keep us from finding God's grace. Before, I was self-
centered and consumed with my imperfections. Now, I was
obsessed with being in a constant state of humility, trying
to always consider others first. I was trying to do good
things for others, feeling that God would reward me for
my good deeds. My biggest obsession remained this: trying
not to enjoy anything that could possibly be considered
worldly.

I picked up the phone and called Sigmund, who was
not yet my husband but whom I'd been seriously dating for
some time. We chatted for a while and then he sensed that
even though I was staying in a beautiful hotel room and
getting ready to do what I love—make music—that something was wrong. He finally asked me outright, "Cindy,
what's wrong?"

So I told him about my struggle. "So you think it is sinful
to enjoy worldly things? You know, things that are not
directly involved with Jesus or leading others to faith?"

He was silent for a moment.

Then he asked me to turn in my Bible to John 3:16.

Ok, I thought. *Where is he going with this?* After all, I
knew this verse like the back of my hand. I could quote
it from memory. What new insight could I possibly gain
from it?

Nonetheless, I opened my Bible and listened as he read
aloud, "For God so loved the world that He gave His only
begotten Son, that whoever believes in Him should not
perish but have everlasting life." And then verse 17, "For
God did not send His Son into the world to condemn the
world, but that the world through Him might be saved."

The words, "so loved the world" jumped off the page at
me. Sigmund said that God created the world for us to

enjoy and that it seemed to him that it would probably make God sad if we went through our whole life without experiencing the wonder and joy of the many gifts He has given us.

I had always struggled with the idea that such "worldly" activities as laughing at a joke with friends, playing the piano, taking a long walk with someone you cared about, or watching a TV show were, in at least some way, sinful.

But as Sigmund read this verse aloud to me and explained what it meant to him, I felt a crack begin to emerge in the dam that was holding back all of my emotions and longings.

I began to thank God for all the simple gifts He had given me, gifts I'd neglected because I didn't think they were "spiritual" enough. I began to understand that God cared about everything in my life, even the nonspiritual elements.

He loved me.

He accepted me as I was.

He wanted me to enjoy the life that He had given His to save.

Bible Thumper

There was a time in my life when it seemed as though my whole life was centered around reading the Bible.

My first act upon waking was to reach over to my nightstand and pull my large, heavy black Bible to my lap and start to read.

Before I went to sleep at night, I'd read the Bible.

Whenever I was traveling, I would read my Bible.

Before every concert, I'd spend time reading the Bible.

In fact, about any time I had a spare moment you could find me reading the Bible.

You may think I'm bragging, or maybe that I'm reminiscing about a time when I was a more committed Christian, but nothing could be further from the truth.

Sure I read the Bible a lot, but I read it out of fear.

I CAN REMEMBER SITTING ON a plane—which is where I have spent a good portion of the last eight years of my life—and watching one of the other passengers reading a novel or a magazine. I felt envious of how content they looked, how much they seemed to be enjoying the simple act of getting lost in a book or an interesting article. Because, to be honest, I wasn't enjoying the time I was spending in the Bible.

How I wished I could feel relaxed enough about my walk with God that I could actually just not think about it for a while.

But at that point in my life I lived with the burden of feeling that every waking moment must be focused only on God and His Word. If I didn't live with this attitude, I assumed that God would be unhappy with me. Wasn't it "worldly" to have any other interest than my spiritual life? I guess I believed that God would punish me if I didn't continually cleanse my mind with His Word.

I thought He might take away something that was precious to me: my voice or my ability to write songs.

When it came right down to it, I believed that pleasure of any sort was sinful, whether it be the pleasure derived from wonderful music, a deep friendship, or any of the other simple joys of living. If I was enjoying life, I had come to believe, I was probably in sin.

Whenever we traveled by bus or van, the guys in the band would bring along favorite books and CDs. They'd be laughing and carefree, talking and enjoying themselves.

Me? I'd be sitting with a knot in my stomach and a Bible on my lap.

Trying to be pleasing to God and feeling so very unhappy.

And feeling paralyzed and inadequate and ruled by fear.

Members of the band would laugh and joke about how spiritual I was, but little did they know how very unhappy

I really was. I couldn't open up and be honest about my struggles. I was always worried about how I could make sure that God remained pleased with me. After all, one wouldn't dare complain about having to read the Bible, right?

But reading the Bible was no longer a privilege and a joy.

It was a prison.

WHERE DID MY ATTITUDE OF obedience based on fear come from? Or the idea that God was only concerned about "spiritual" things?

I remember that as I was growing up, my mother would never read anything except the Bible or devotional books. She had little time for anything that wasn't "spiritual." I guess I picked up some of her obsessiveness. But thinking back on it now, I'm not sure she ever really found much of God's joy in any of her reading. It seemed to be mostly about duty and fear and not very much about grace. She seemed to be looking for something she never found in the pages of her Bible.

It was there to be found, but her focus on trying to please God got in the way of letting Him love her.

MY DAD, ON THE OTHER HAND, loved to read a variety of things—fiction, history, etc. He used his books to educate himself far beyond his six years of schooling. To him, the Bible was an important book, but God taught him through his other reading as well.

Only now am I learning the full wisdom of Dad's approach. That God intends us to find love and meaning and joy in our relationship with Him. That He will be our companion through all the adventures of life, walking beside and with us, making *everything* in our lives holy—not just the religious things.

So why do I read the Bible?

Is it because I am afraid not to? That I will be somehow punished for my neglect? That I have to live up to the expectations of others in regard to my spirituality?

Or is it because I want to.

Because of the joy I find in meeting God in His Word.

If you read God's Word because you love it and crave it, you'll find the peace that comes from finding Him in its pages. If you read only out of duty and fear, the peace you seek will always elude you.

Practicing spiritual disciplines like Bible reading and prayer is a little like marriage. Imagine if you married a man because he had threatened to harm you if you didn't. Wouldn't that throw a taint over your life with him? Would you ever be able to love him in a free and wondrous way? Would you ever be able to grasp that love and commitment come by choice, not by force?

Many struggle—as I did—with a distorted concept of God. A God who has expectations that are simply too high for me to be able to meet, a God whom I can never please or satisfy, who is angry when anything other than Him has any real importance in our lives.

How can we undo the false face of God that so many of us see in our minds when we pray or dream or fall into sin? How can we undo the damage and start over?

For me, coming to an understanding of the God who really loves me meant starting over; letting one journey with God end so another might begin.

I had to become a child all over again and relearn who God was and how He felt about me.

That I could be nurtured and taught by the hand of a loving Father.

That even when I make mistakes or am not all I should be I am accepted and loved unconditionally.

That in His Word I could find strength and hope to control my fear. That reading the Bible could be fun and exciting. That it could set my spirit free.

Although I don't read the Bible nearly as much as I need to—and when I say "need to" it is because the words have the ability when read with the right understanding to bring peace, joy, and a new way of living. I would be less than honest if I did not tell you that I am still in search of the balance I need to see the Bible for what it truly is—a doorway that leads you out of the darkness and into a new world.

Lula

Bridge Over Nothingness

In my dream I am on a narrow bridge that stretches over a yawning canyon whose sides slip steeply away opposite each other. I am making my way from one side to the other. But as I reach the halfway point on my journey, suddenly there is no longer a bridge under my feet—it has ended midway across the chasm.

And then I see myself falling, my body spinning slowly as it plunges toward the muddy waters below. I cannot swim to safety.

I know I will die in these murky waters.

As a little girl I dreamt this nightmare scenario on repeated occasions, awakening each time with fear and terror.

It instilled in me a fear of bridges and of deep water—especially water that isn't clear. But I know inside myself that it isn't really the bridges and water that I am afraid of.

It is something deeper.

Deeper than the daily struggles with fear that I have shared in this book. On a good day, when the sun is shining and I am feeling peaceful enough to be honest with myself, my soul whispers the truth to me.

The thing I have always feared most is death.

DEATH RAISES QUESTIONS. How will we meet our final demise? What awaits us on the other side?

To be honest, I cannot fully grasp the idea of my spirit traveling beyond my body and beginning a journey into eternity. It's too big an idea for me to fully comprehend. I struggle to make sense of it all.

You may be wondering—how can it be right for a Christian to fear death in light of what the Bible tells us lies before us? We are promised streets of gold. And crystal rivers…

I believe in my heart that God is real and heaven will be all it is promised to be. It will be real.

But I have never seen or touched it.

It is not real to me in the same way that a daisy is real.

It is not real to me in the same way that the miracle of love is real.

Yet it is just such realities as a daisy and a lingering hug that fill me with love and wonder. They remind me of the Power behind all things. The Power that causes the earth to spin in its orbit and the caterpillar to emerge from its chrysalis as a butterfly.

He has everything in control.

The things I understand.

And the things I don't understand.

THERE WILL BE A MOMENT WHEN I will leave this earth and all the things I love about it. And I will go to an unknown place. God promises that on the other side of death is a better place. Someday, when my body is weak and my bones are tired, I will be ready to embrace the life that waits beyond.

It will be wonderful to close my eyes here and awaken on the other side.

To see my father's sweet and smiling face.

To laugh again with Samuel and other loved ones who left this world before me.

To know that all my fears were in vain and that God's love is even more wondrous than I could ever have imagined. To know that He is my bridge over the chasm of my fears.

January Snow

Today is January 2.

I'm looking out my window at a world covered in a blanket of freshly fallen white snow. The mailman is making his rounds, accompanied by the sound of barking dogs.

All over the neighborhood, people have stripped their Christmas trees of ornaments and dragged them into their front yards, awaiting pickup by the garbage man. They are now only bare and browned remnants of their recent glory.

And I feel kinda sad.

Sad that another Christmas season has passed. Sad that it will be another year before the joy of family and friends and holiday goodies will be experienced again.

I love Christmastime.

STARING AT THE BROWN Christmas trees, I am carried back in memory to earlier times and to a lesson I learned one Christmas when I was a child.

113

We lived in the hollow (pronounced "holler" if you live in the South) in that small cabin I wrote about earlier—all seven of us. Although money was never plentiful, it was a great place to grow up.

During the Christmas season, Dad and I would go into the woods with Bear, our big ugly dog, and chop wood all day.

Evenings, we'd sit in front of the fire, telling stories and roasting marshmallows.

Sometimes, when there was a lot of snow, Dad would tie an innertube to the back of our Volkswagen Bug and give my sisters and me a high-speed sleigh ride around the nearby field.

We had little money, but we were rich in love.

ONE EVENING, A FEW DAYS before Christmas, Dad came home with several empty baskets and a box full of fruit, nuts, and candy. His idea was to make fruit baskets for our neighbors.

(Although the prospect of making the baskets seemed like a grand little adventure, my young mind couldn't help but wonder who would want a dumb old fruit basket as a Christmas gift! It didn't sound like something I'd want!)

We filled the baskets and made the rounds. Everyone seemed genuinely pleased with them and thanked us warmly. There was only one last stop to make—a stop I wasn't especially looking forward to.

The final family on our list was the Hoskins, who lived in a nearby holler. Mr. and Mrs. Hoskins had two boys, both adopted. Their names were Billy Ray and Otis, and they both had sandy blond hair and brown eyes. I remember seeing Otis dressed up one time and thinking that he almost looked cute, but most of the time the two boys were dirty from all the work they did outside and smelly from the lack of a good long bath.

I always felt sorry for them when we drove by their home. The front yard was filled with all sorts of garbage and littered with two or three beat-up old cars that didn't look as if they'd been driven any time recently.

Their house was dilapidated and chickens ran free on the porch, leaving behind the telltale signs of their presence: feathers, manure, and an unpleasant smell. Their home had few modern conveniences. Because they had no indoor plumbing, they had to use an outhouse located about a hundred yards from their house.

All this made me feel badly for them, but what really made me sad was seeing how lonely Billy Ray and Otis always looked. It was no surprise they were that way. Their mother yelled at them constantly, telling them they were worthless and stupid. Their father was the kind of man who didn't say much at all. He certainly didn't contradict his wife as she drove them into the ground with her criticism.

But what really defeated the boys—more than the harsh words or the scars from one too many beatings—was the fact that they never received any outward manifestation of love. No words of encouragement or praise or comfort.

They would get few elsewhere either, for people tended to shy away from the Hoskinses.

So Dad made a point to reach out to that sad family.

And they were so very grateful.

They gathered breathlessly around the basket, handling each item in it as if we had given them gold rather than fruit and nuts. You could tell they were moved beyond words.

When we drove away, the Hoskinses all stood together on their porch and waved until we were out of sight.

REMEMBERING THAT DAY ON THIS cold January morning so many years later, I think that maybe what moved them was not the gift itself, but the act of giving and the love behind it.

I think that maybe what my dad wanted them to see was this:

When you have Christ inside, even the angriest heart or most wounded soul can come to the tree of forgiveness and find new life.

Today, looking at the brown tree in my own front yard, I am reminded that there is always a Billy Ray or Otis to reach out to. Not just at Christmastime, but all year round.

And I am filled with a sense of renewed joy that in this new year there is still a tree that we can cling to. One that will never lose its needles or fade to brown—the tree of Calvary that Jesus died on to make a way for us. At that tree even the blackest of hearts can stand before Him and be made white.

Just like January snow.

Sounds of Denial

Sometimes my mother chooses the oddest times to decide to discuss theology.

I am standing in a sea of people at the Las Vegas airport, surrounded by multitudes of arriving and departing travelers. The air is filled with the clanging and ringing of slot machines. Wouldn't you know it; Las Vegas even has slot machines in the airport. They are noisy and distracting.

My cell phone is glued to my ear, straining to hear my mother on the other end of the line as she tells me about some messianic Bible studies she has been attending. Out of the blue she fires off several questions—one of which is whom I believe Jesus to be.

"Mom, I'm standing in the middle of an airport, surrounded by people, waiting for my luggage. I don't think this is a very good time to get into this."

She persists in asking me. I repeat my original response.

I can hear her sigh on the other end, and I take the opportunity to change the subject, hoping to stop her from pressing the question again.

PICTURE ANOTHER scene.

A man is separated from his traveling companions in a strange and dangerous city. He warms his hands over a fire. The others gathered round discuss the capture of a troublemaker in town. One of them gives the unfamiliar face a second look.

"Hey, you are one of the ones who was with Him."

The man denies it.

"Listen to the way he talks," someone else chimes in, "he's straight from the shores of Galilee."

He denies it again with more vehemence. And then, pressed further, he shouts out his denial.

In the distance he hears a rooster crow and remembers the prediction of his friend and Master: "Peter, you will deny Me three times…"

IT IS EASY TO SIT HERE SO MANY centuries later and feel smug, confident that if you or I were in the same position at the fire, we would have gladly stood by Jesus. That unlike Peter, we would not have deserted a friend in His time of need.

Peter's life was in danger. The threat involved in associating with Jesus was very real.

But how many times do we deny Jesus daily, when there is no threat worse than the possibility of a little embarrassment?

We fear being seen to be fanatical—a Bible thumper— some sort of outcast from polite society.

Standing there in the Las Vegas airport, if I had listened closely, I too might have heard the sound of a rooster crowing in the distance above the sounds of flight announcements and the ringing of the ever-present slot machines.

I was too embarrassed to get into a conversation with my mother about Jesus.

WHEN A FRIEND STRETCHES OUT a prayer of grace just a little too long at a restaurant, and you feel the eyes of others upon you, do you secretly wish the person praying would just hurry up and get to the amen?

Are you shy about being caught reading the Bible in public?

Do you expend great effort not to let it be too clear to people just how dedicated you are to your faith and your Savior?

I HAVE TO ASK MYSELF THIS QUESTION: How many times have I denied the Lord for silly and trivial reasons?

Jesus knows our weaknesses and He sees our hearts.

He knew Peter. He knew me in the airport.

He knows how often we will fail Him.

He knows, too, how much we need Him.

Which is why He came.

Mom and me backstage

A Smile, Some Salsa, and a Green Bike

He smiled at me through the part between his front teeth and asked, "Would you like some salsa?"

I was in Los Angeles on business and found myself with a free evening, so I decided to take in some shopping at the Beverly Center, a beautiful glass and marble shopping center. I was relaxed and not in a hurry at all. I took my time wandering through all the stores, looking for a few bargains. When my stomach started to rumble, I realized I hadn't eaten in a while, so I went in search of some fast food.

A few minutes later I was leaning against the counter of La Salsa, giving my order to a very unhappy young girl wearing a uniform, a red apron, and a frown.

She shouted my order to the cook in Spanish, requesting a classic cheese quesadilla with guacamole on the side.

While they prepared my order, I found a table in the food court and set my bags down. I asked a woman sitting nearby if she would mind watching my stuff for a moment. She agreed.

Looking up, I noticed a Dairy Queen sign and realized that I *needed* some sort of treat. I sauntered over to that counter and gave my order to a young guy dressed in his happy-looking uniform.

"I'll have a small Reese's Peanut Butter Blizzard, please."

"I'm sorry, we are out of that flavor," he said.

"Ok," I answered, hesitating a moment over my second choice. "How about a Butterfinger Blizzard, then?"

"Great," he said as he rang up the order. "I'll give you 50 cents off since we didn't have your first selection."

We stood there smiling, both of us happy about this small token of kindness.

I thanked him and went back over to La Salsa to pick up my quesadilla.

That's when the friendly guy with the space in his smile asked, "Would you like some salsa?"

"Yes, please."

As I reached across the counter he smiled a dazzling smile and said, "Enjoy."

I stood there a moment, almost overcome by the urge to reach across the counter and give him a big hug. He seemed so happy to do his job, taking pleasure in being able to give a little extra. Even if it was only salsa.

I THOUGHT ABOUT MY OWN tendency to be selfish, my own reluctance to share. It is easy to forget how much joy can be found in giving.

Even if it is only an extra M&M or letting someone ahead of you in traffic or a smile and some extra salsa.

The joy of giving was something my father knew.

I REMEMBER MY ELEVENTH birthday.

I remember gazing into the sweet face of my father, who was trying to explain to me that he wasn't able to afford very much for my birthday, but that he did have a little something.

My dad supported five kids with his job as a VW mechanic. There was never enough money for designer clothes. We always had the Wal-Mart version of what was hip that year. There wasn't money for a lot of extras.

I followed him out the screen door on that hot, steamy day in early June.

As we rounded the corner of our house, I caught my first glimpse of something wonderful in the middle of the backyard. There, adorned with a yellow ribbon, was a bike.

The bike was bright green.

On closer inspection I understood how he had managed such a wonderful gift in such a lean year.

Dad had gone to the junkyard and found parts from an old bike that had been tossed away, probably by some boy who was getting a new dirt bike. The original color of the beat-up old bike was dark blue, but my dad saw it and had a vision for what it could be.

He patiently waded through a sea of broken toys, tires, and scattered parts until he found all the necessary items for his recipe. Over the course of a few weeks, he found time after hours to work on it in the garage. He fixed the broken and damaged parts, patched the holes in the tires, sanded the frame, and made sure every nut and bolt was tightly in place.

Then it was ready for a coat of paint. He selected the color both of us loved: green.

A bright, blinding green.

It was perfect.

I JUMPED ON THE SEAT LIKE the bike was a stallion.

And the adventure began.

I sped around the gravel cul-de-sac in our neighborhood, skinning my legs and knees every time I tried to go too fast and turn too tightly. Which was often.

Sometimes I would tie my favorite superhero beach towel around my neck, letting it flow down my back all the way to my ankles. Then I would trudge to the top of the little hill in our backyard and ride down as fast as I could, my Converse tennis shoes working those pedals with all my might.

I came flying down off that hill with the breeze lifting my hair and my Wonder Woman cape trailing out behind me. Turning slightly, I'd swoop under the snowball tree, letting its magical petals drift down on me in a blizzard of white.

My love affair with that bike lasted many years.

Then, one summer, we moved away from our little white house.

Away from the gravel road, the little backyard hill, and the snowball tree.

Somewhere in the move my bike was either overlooked or purposely thrown out.

I never found it again.

There are days when I would give anything to feel the handlebars of that old green bike and taste again the magic that it brought into my life during my very own wonder years.

I THOUGHT ABOUT THIS IN THE MALL as I glanced over at the lady who had watched my bags and noticed that she was sharing an order of fries with her tiny little daughter. The girl reminds me of myself at her age, with dark ringlets of hair cascading around a happy but bewildered face.

They laugh and talk as they eat their fries.

I wonder if perhaps they could only afford one order of fries between them. Whatever the case, the joy they share is a palpable as the scent of fries that hangs in the air. I hope—that just like my father—this woman always finds time for her daughter.

Time passes so quickly.

My father was always so kind. He always had time for us.

Time that has now slipped away like river water running through my hands.

LA SALSA IS TURNING THEIR lights off. The man with the smile and the salsa is going home.

The lady and her daughter are walking away hand in hand.

And almost two decades later, it is June 4—and my birthday once again. And I wish there were some sort of time machine that could take me back to that day so long ago.

To the backyard, the bike, the snowball tree, and the eyes of a father who gave me the most priceless of gifts—his love.

Shelter in the Storm

My sister, Sam, had a recurring nightmare that she once shared with me.

In the nightmare she was inside her home feeling warm, snug, and safe. The air was filled with the smell of cookies baking in the kitchen and the hum of a game on television in the living room, where her husband snoozed in the recliner. She could hear the children's laughter as they played in their rooms.

Then, in the kitchen window appeared a beautiful face, peering in from outside. It was the face of an angel, glowing and white.

He spoke to her in whispered tones that seemed to echo in her head. His voice was like a melodious mist that cast a spell and weaved a web around her senses.

"Come outside," he whispered, "I have something beautiful to show you."

Feeling compelled, she took slow, methodical steps until she reached the door, where she saw him in the distance.

His arms were outstretched, welcoming her, motioning her to come.

But as she drew nearer, the vision morphed into something horrific. His arms grew longer until they reached into the sky like a twisting vapor. The face, once beautiful, became fearsome as it laughed with a menacing glee. Then the body of the angel became a funnel, dark and deep, which ripped through her home, destroying everything in sight as she stood there frozen in terror.

It is not surprising that Sam would have a dream like this.

Growing up in eastern Tennessee, there were many tornadoes that came very close to our house.

I remember spending a long, scary night in the cellar when one came within a mile of our home. We grabbed blankets, lanterns, and some snacks and descended into the cellar. The concrete walls and floor of the cellar were damp and uninviting, but there were bunks built into the wall for sleeping.

As though I would actually be able to sleep through this frightening night!

In addition to the threat of the tornado outside was my fear of the creepy, crawly things that inhabited the cellar but we couldn't see because of the darkness.

Even now, I get sweaty palms just thinking about that night.

Now, many years later, I spend a great deal of the year living in a small prairie town in Alberta, Canada.

When I first began dating Sigmund, I paid him a visit in his hometown. During a walk in the woods on a lovely summer day, he noticed I was watching the ground in front of me as I walked.

"Why are you staring at your feet?" he asked.

"I'm not," I replied. "I'm watching for snakes."

He chuckled and said, "There are several advantages to living in Alberta. Among them are the absence of rats, poisonous spiders, tornadoes, and snakes. Apparently the winter is too long and too cold for them to survive it. As for tornadoes...well, we just never have them."

So, I thought, *while everyone else in the world is experiencing tornadoes, hurricanes, and earthquakes, things remain pretty calm and unchanging in the beautiful prairies of Alberta.*

But this last summer, as we were leaving to meet Sigmund's parents for dinner, we heard that a storm was approaching. So we closed the house up tight before we left. After dinner, upon leaving the restaurant, we heard people talking about a tornado. We rushed to the car and turned the radio on.

Pine Lake—just eight miles from our house—had been struck by a massive tornado. Twenty lives had been lost at Green Acres Campground and three or four hundred people had been injured.

That week, after the first tornado, four other tornadoes touched down in the areas surrounding us.

For several nights after the tornado, I would stare out the large window in our living room, every cloud looking black and menacing, and imagine the face in my sister's dream. I had to fight the urge to run down to the basement.

So much for my husband's assurances...

FEAR CAN HAVE SO MANY FACES.

Creaks in the floor, monsters under the bed, angels that turn into tornadoes.

We can never really escape from the things that cause us to be afraid. For every one we secure ourselves against, there will be another waiting to take its place.

The world is not under our control.

So it all comes down to learning to trust God. We often cannot do very much to change our circumstances, but we can do something about how we respond to them. When the tornadoes in our lives threaten us, will we surrender to fear (a response that does little good in terms of actually dealing with the threat) or will we lay our fear in the hands of the One who loves us?

It helps just then to remember His promise that He will never leave or forsake us. The more I grow to trust Him, the more I find Him to be my shelter in the storm.

Morning Has Broken

Do you remember the first days of summer?

The sun smiles into your window, beckoning you to come outside.

Running, jumping, diving into a pool of cool water.

Complete freedom. Your legs seem as though they will never tire and you feel as though you'll never be out of breath.

Today I have awakened to just such a feeling.

THE ARIZONA SUN IS SLANTING through my window, awakening me and making me wish I was a child again. Instead, I am with child. Almost six months pregnant.

I know that my legs could only run so far before the weight of the miracle growing inside me would slow me down.

When I stare into the faces of nieces, six and seven years old, I am reminded of what it is to be a child, filled with wonder and taking pleasure in all the little gifts God has hidden within each and every moment.

Their eyes are so alive, their golden hair falls in waves down their backs, their smiles seem unquenchable. I long to be as free as they are. To take that kind of joy in living. To be that free from fear.

I am learning to be free from some of the chains that wrap themselves around my soul.

This freedom is surely just a hint of what God has prepared for me.

Crossing Over

Writing this book has been like walking back through the pages of my life. It has been interesting to relive the experiences and emotions of my past as I've set them down in lines of printed prose.

The one truth that has impressed itself on me is this: I've changed.

Sometimes as I wrote out my reflections it was as if God was shining a new and healing light on my past. When I finished writing some of the stories I had to tear them up and try again. They seemed inadequate somehow. In the process of writing itself, I've gained new perspectives on my life.

God continues to help me understand myself and the path on which He is leading me.

I guess what is important to me is to remain open to being taught something new. To be always ready to change my views, even about things I thought I was sure of.

I find it eventful and important to tell you that, in the last stages of writing this book, my mother—whom I have shared so much about—had an overwhelming spiritual breakthrough in her life. I am so proud of her for having the courage to face all the pain she has endured in her own journey to find a new way of life. One that is free of guilt, pain, and fear.

For the pain and grief in our lives can make us bitter. It can make us close ourselves up in a safe cocoon of our own construction.

The pain and grief in our lives can make us think we are wiser than we really are. What may feel like the well-earned knowledge of experience may only be protective self-defense or fear. We may understand much less than we think, having only scratched the surface of the things that really matter.

I'll be honest with you—I still struggle with some of my fears.

But they no longer rule my life.

I am learning how to walk with God, trying to discover the balance between my own desires and those God has placed within my heart. I am learning how to trust Him and look for the small beauties that surround me rather than anticipating the worst in every situation.

Overcoming fear is a process.

I've learned to look at my life as a journey.

But on the path I walk I know this: The dark valleys I have crossed have made the smallest of mountains seem even more glorious.

I like the view from higher ground.

THESE DAYS I LIVE IN AN OLD-FASHIONED farmhouse. It is surrounded by meadows of golden wheat and is perched high upon a hill.

From here I can see hawks soaring and deer grazing.

At night I can hear the howling of coyotes in the distance.

A short walk from our house leads to a field where Saskatoon berries grow in the midst of the bursting colors of wildflowers. The berries are sweet and delicious.

Wouldn't you know—between me and that field of berries and wildflowers is a tall barbed wire fence. I smile to think about how life tends to travel in a circle, always bringing us back to our fears and longings.

Sometimes I have been caught on the sharp edges while trying to squeeze through between the wires. They have cut me. They have made me bleed.

But I will not let that deter me from the beauty that lies beyond.

I still wear shoes whenever I know I'll be crossing the fence.

But there will come a day when the sun is warm and the air is clean, when I will let go of my fears and inhibitions, flinging off my sandals, and feeling the cool grass between my toes.

I will walk to that old fence and cross over...

Barefoot on barbed wire.

Appendix:
Some Bible Passages on Fear

ON THE NEXT SEVERAL PAGES I'd like to share with you some Scriptures that have been very helpful to me in my battle against fear. If you will read them and make them part of your life I'm sure you'll find them to be a great help and comfort when you feel assaulted by feelings of fear.

PSALM 91

He who dwells in the secret place of the Most High shall abide under the shadow of the Almighty.

I will say of the LORD, "He is my refuge and my fortress; My God, in Him I will trust."

Surely He shall deliver you from the snare of the fowler and from the perilous pestilence. He shall cover you with His feathers, and under His wings you shall take refuge; His truth shall be your shield and buckler.

You shall not be afraid of the terror by night, nor of the arrow that flies by day, nor of the pestilence that walks in darkness, nor of the destruction that lays waste at noonday.

A thousand may fall at your side, and ten thousand at your right hand; but it shall not come near you.

Only with your eyes shall you look, and see the reward of the wicked. Because you have made the LORD, who is my refuge, even the Most High, your dwelling place, no evil shall befall you, nor shall any plague come near your dwelling; for He shall give His angels charge over you, to keep you in all your ways. In their hands they shall bear you up, lest you dash your foot against a stone.

You shall tread upon the lion and the cobra, the young lion and the serpent you shall trample underfoot.

"Because he has set his love upon Me, therefore I will deliver him; I will set him on high, because he has known My name. He shall call upon Me, and I will answer him; I will be with him in trouble; I will deliver him and honor him. With long life I will satisfy him, and show him My salvation."

JOSHUA 1:2-5

"Moses My servant is dead. Now therefore, arise, go over this Jordan, you and all this people, to the land which I am giving to them—the children of Israel. Every place that the sole of your foot will tread upon I have given you, as I said to Moses.

"From the wilderness and this Lebanon as far as the great river, the River Euphrates, all the land of the Hittites, and to the Great Sea toward the going down of the sun, shall be your territory.

"No man shall be able to stand before you all the days of your life; as I was with Moses, so I will be with you. I will not leave you nor forsake you."

1 CHRONICLES 28:20

And David said to his son Solomon, "Be strong and of good courage, and do it; do not fear nor be dismayed, for the LORD God—my God—will be with you. He will not leave you nor forsake you, until you have finished all the work for the service of the house of the LORD."

PSALM 27:1-5

The LORD is my light and my salvation; whom shall I fear? The LORD is the strength of my life; of whom shall I be afraid?

When the wicked came against me to eat up my flesh, my enemies and foes, they stumbled and fell.

Though an army may encamp against me, my heart shall not fear; though war should rise against me, in this I will be confident.

One thing I have desired of the LORD, that will I seek: That I may dwell in the house of the LORD all the days of my life, to behold the beauty of the LORD, and to inquire in His temple.

For in the time of trouble He shall hide me in His pavilion; in the secret place of His tabernacle He shall hide me; He shall set me high upon a rock.

MARK 4:38-40

But He was in the stern, asleep on a pillow. And they awoke Him and said to Him, "Teacher, do You not care that we are perishing?"

Then He arose and rebuked the wind, and said to the sea, "Peace, be still!" And the wind ceased and there was a great calm.

But He said to them, "Why are you so fearful? How is it that you have no faith?"

LUKE 9:24,25

For whoever desires to save his life will lose it, but whoever loses his life for My sake will save it. For what profit is it to a man if he gains the whole world, and is himself destroyed or lost?

2 TIMOTHY 1:6,7

Therefore I remind you to stir up the gift of God which is in you through the laying on of my hands. For God has not given us a spirit of fear, but of power and of love and of a sound mind.

Favorite Writing Spot
in the holler

Cindy Morgan not only penned this book, but she has also recorded several incredible records. Be sure to check out Cindy's music on any one of the following CDs, all available on Word Records:

- The Best So Far
- The Loving Kind
- Listen
- Under the Waterfall
- A Reason to Live
- Real Life

And for the latest news on Cindy Morgan, go to www.wordrecords.com!

Other Good
Harvest House Reading

Living the Questions
Carolyn Arends

Striking a chord that resonates with anyone who has asked the "whys" and "what ifs" of faith, Carolyn Arends shares portions of her life and walk that offer insights into why God weaves His way into the mundane moments of our lives.

Blessed Are the Desperate for They Will Find Hope
Bonnie Keen

Bonnie Keen's life turned upside down: Her husband left her, she struggled with clinical depression, and she nearly lost her music ministry. At the end of her rope, she learned that when the whole world seems to fall apart, God can put the pieces back together again.

The Power of a Praying™ Wife
Stormie Omartian

Stormie shares how wives can develop a deeper relationship with their husbands by praying for them. Packed with practical advice on praying for specific areas, including decision-making, fears, spiritual strength, and sexuality, women will discover the fulfilling marriage God intended.

Ragamuffin Prayers
Ragamuffin Band/Jimmy Abegg

You will be encouraged by these thoughts on prayer and how God uses our imperfections to accomplish His will. Contributors include The Ragamuffin Band, Michael W. Smith, and Brennan Manning. Includes photos.